The beginnings of Birmingham City Football Club have always been poorly documented. The customary line that a group of Trinity Church cricketers originally started the club to keep themselves together during the winter months has long been the extent of the narrative. But who were these cricketers, and what is their story?

After five years of research, author David Ely has managed to piece events together to build a thought provoking account of the founders' early lives and the club's formative years from 1875 to 1888 – the forgotten Small Heath Alliance era. His determination to find out what happened was fired by previous research into his own family history, which revealed that at the time of the 1871 census, his great-great-grandfather, Frederick Ely, was living in the same street (Cattel Road) as several founding players. He was aware that Frederick had experienced hard times in Small Heath, including a spell in prison and a lingering demise in the workhouse after contracting TB, and was now more intrigued than ever to find out more about the club's first players and their own experiences.

David Ely was born and brought up in Birmingham, and started watching the Blues in the late 1960s. He now lives with his wife in South Devon.

IN SEARCH OF
SMALL HEATH ALLIANCE

THE FORGOTTEN PIONEERS OF BIRMINGHAM CITY 1875 TO 1888

DAVID ELY

OLD BOOTS PUBLISHING

First published in the UK by Old Boots Publishing, Devon

Copyright © David Ely 2017
The moral right of the author has been asserted

All rights reserved
This book is sold subject to the condition that it may not, by way of trade or otherwise, be lent, resold, hired out or otherwise be circulated without the publisher's prior consent in any form of binding or cover other than that in which it is published and without a similar condition including this condition being imposed on the subsequent purchaser

ISBN 978 1 5272 1010 3

Printed and bound in Great Britain by
Short Run Press Limited, Exeter, Devon

For dear Florence

ACKNOWLEDGEMENTS

Firstly, I want to thank my pals Phil and Derek Smith, who along with their dad, gave me my first chance to see the Blues in the late 1960s, which immediately became a regular thing. In those days, like most other fans, we went by bus. For us it was a number 55 bus from Shard End to Saltley Gate, where we jumped onto one of the numerous football specials that were queuing ready to take the hordes to St. Andrews. I was immediately hooked, and without this initial experience, this book would never have materialised, albeit nearly fifty years afterwards.

Thanks also go to my good friend Richard Wood for kindly allowing me to use two photographs that he took in Small Heath in the 1970s of the Plume of Feathers pub in Miles Street, and the New Inn in Muntz Street.

On the other side of the world, I was helped by Andrew McNiven, an employee of the New Zealand Post Limited in Wellington, NZ, who kindly tracked down some details for me of Alliance founder David Keys at the NZ National Archives in Wellington.

Thanks also to Gordon Taylor OBE, Chief Executive of the Professional Footballers' Association, for his kind endorsement of the book.

Finally, I could not have finished this book without the unswerving support of my dear wife, who encouraged me through the natural ups and downs of my quest, even though it meant that I was often preoccupied with my research, and many a time only had one topic of conversation.

CONTENTS

	Page No.
1. So Many Unanswered Questions	1
2. Small Heath before Football	3
3. The Cricket Converts - Exploring how Association Football first emerged in Birmingham	8
4. The Small Heath Alliance club is up and running	17
5. The birth of the Birmingham and District Football Association and it's power struggle with the Aston Lower Grounds Company	30
6. Early Developments at Small Heath Alliance 1876 to 1878	36
6.1 The Summer of 1876	36
6.2 One Season at Ladypool Lane 1876/77	38
6.3 The Return to Small Heath at Gessey's Field 1877	46
7. Progress gathers pace 1878 to 1881	49
7.1 First Competitive Fixture 1878/79	49
7.2 The Alliance cause a seismic Cup shock 1879/80	54
7.3 Muntz Street's First Four Figure Crowd 1880/81	61
8. Football Fever in the early 1880s	66
8.1 The Rise of Junior Football in Small Heath	66
8.2 Cup Mania at the Alliance 1881/82	68
8.3 Francis Henry Crittall; An Alliance man from 1882 who went on to fame and fortune	76
9. The First Trophy; A Triumph in Adversity 1882/83	78
9.1 Replacing Billy Edden	78
9.2 New Blood from Potter's Field	79

9.3 The First Player to turn out for both the Alliance and Villa	81
9.4 Shocking Events at Ruabon	82
9.5 The Victorious Walsall Cup Campaign 1882/83	85
10. The Alliance Strive to Keep Pace 1883 to 1885	**92**
10.1 A New Breed of Administrator	92
10.2 An Adventurous Fixture List 1883/84	94
10.3 "The Great Local Match"	98
10.4 Recruitment of New Talent	99
10.5 Professionalism in the Air 1884/85	105
10.6 Three Epic Encounters at Muntz Street	106
11. The Start of the Professional Era 1885/86	**110**
11.1 How the Alliance Coped with Professionalism	110
11.2 The Alliance's Storming F.A. Cup Run	114
11.3 Rivalry with Aston Villa Ignited	121
12. On the Financial Treadmill 1886 to 1888	**124**
12.1 Alf "Inky" Jones Elected Honorary Secretary	124
12.2 Challenging Times 1886/87	125
12.3 The move to "Limited Company" status 1887/88	132
12.4 The World's First Football Club Shareholders 1888	137

Appendix 1 List of Small Heath Alliance competitive matches
Appendix 2 List of Alliance players' representative games
Appendix 3 Club Captains
Appendix 4 Honorary Secretaries
Reference Sources

FOREWORD
by Gordon Taylor OBE

As a lover of football history with very fond memories of my time with Birmingham City in the 70s, it is a real pleasure to recommend this book by Dave Ely on the origins of the club and those early pioneers responsible for the "birth of the Blues!"

About Gordon Taylor

Gordon Taylor made more than 200 appearances for the Blues, playing as a direct and tenacious winger. He was signed from Bolton Wanderers in December 1970 during manager Freddie Goodwin's first season in charge, in what was to be a highly successful five year period. His debut against Carlisle United coincided with Trevor Francis's run of 14 goals in 13 games as a sixteen year old.

Then in the following season (1971/72), Gordon was a pivotal member of the Blues team which gained promotion to the top tier of English football. Later he was to suffer the disappointment of losing in two F.A. Cup semi-finals, first against Leeds United in 1972, and again in 1975, after a replay, against a Bobby Moore and Alan Mullery inspired Fulham team.

Gordon's involvement with the PFA started in 1972 while he was at the Blues, when he was appointed onto the PFA Management Committee, keeping company with fellow players such as Terry Venables and Bobby Charlton. He became boss of the PFA in 1981.

1
SO MANY UNANSWERED QUESTIONS

On the 22nd May 1939 the life of a frail old man came to a tragic end at his East Finchley home in north London. He had found his middle aged daughter, Winnifred, slumped lifeless in her gas filled bedroom, having taken her own life. Shocked and overcome by the choking gas fumes, he was too feeble to save himself. After collapsing in the bedroom doorway, the eighty-one year old man sadly never regained consciousness.

This was how Charles Richmond Barmore, the last surviving member of Small Heath Alliance's founding football team of 1875, sadly passed away. Yet he had remained anonymous to the club he had helped to create, since leaving the Small Heath area in 1883, initially to work as a cycle maker in Coventry. His death had taken with him the last opportunity to gather first hand details of the club's earliest days. Over the years the club and local sporting press had been neglectful in gathering and recording information from founding players, with recollections and memories fading away with each player's passing.

When the Blues made it through to their first F.A. Cup final in 1931, four founding players were still alive; Billy and George Edden, Billy Edmonds and Charlie Barmore. Yet even the occasion of the Cup Final didn't seem to rouse the club or local journalists into seeking them out, and getting their story. Admittedly in Charlie Barmore's case, he had moved away over fifty years earlier, and no one could have been blamed for losing track of his whereabouts, but the other three founders were still living in streets close to the club. It's a telling illustration of how the club's early history was casually allowed to slip from living memory, and be lost forever. Whether this was carelessness, or more a reflection of the relative lack of weightiness given to the subject, is hard to fathom. Whatever the reason, looking back it now seems ill-judged and short-sighted. As a consequence, generations of Blues fans have been left with a gaping hole on how the club first started and developed during the amateur era.

It's unlikely that, in their advancing years, any of the surviving founders managed to venture to the Cup Final, but it still leaves the intriguing prospect of them listening to it on the radio. The 1931 Wembley Final was the fifth to be broadcast, at a time when the proportion of households with radios had risen to nearly a third. The top radio commentator was George Allison, and to help the listener to picture the game, the Radio Times supplied a diagram of the pitch divided into eight numbered squares.

During the commentary, an assistant would constantly call out the square number to indicate the position of the ball.

Fifty-six years earlier, the four survivors had been part of Small Heath Alliance's first football encounter, played on a piece of wasteland next to Arthur Street in the heart of Small Heath. Much of the adjoining land had already been built on, but the bunch of resourceful team mates from the neighbouring streets, used their local knowledge to commandeer the remnants of an old field for their club's first football fixture. Their opponents on that cold afternoon in November 1875 were Holte Wanderers, another rookie team, who had walked up from their Aston Park neighbourhood, just a couple of miles away. There was no fanfare, or any great interest in proceedings from the local residents, and no hint that the game would signal the start of an enduring sporting legacy for Birmingham.

The match ended in a 1-1 draw, and the team sheet, as listed in the club's own centenary publication, *One Hundred Years History of Birmingham City Football Club* (1975) was:

> Will Edden
> A. Wright
> F. James
> T. James
> Geo. Edden
> W.H. Edmunds
> Tom Edden
> David Keys
> C. Barmore
> C. Barr
> J. Sparrow

These were the first "Blue Boys" and without their initial efforts and groundbreaking endeavours the modern club of Birmingham City would not exist today, yet surprisingly the centenary publication didn't seem to have much detail about the club's formative amateur years, or even the first name of every founder.

This book aims to fill the void of information, delving into various aspects of the Alliance club's history, including the early lives of the founding players, the challenges they faced and the club's progress and achievements between 1875 and 1888. To help understand the local football landscape experienced by the early players, the book also explores how football was first popularised in Birmingham, and the reason why the Sheffield Rules version of the game was originally adopted by the local F.A. Many previously undiscovered events and details are recorded.

2
SMALL HEATH BEFORE FOOTBALL

When builder Thomas Edden, and his wife Sarah, moved from Stratford-on-Avon in the late 1840s, they had no idea of the impact it was destined to have on the future sporting landscape of Birmingham. They finally settled in Small Heath in 1852, having moved the mile or so from Rea Street in Digbeth, the birthplace of their first son, William. The family was switching to a newly built home in Mount Pleasant, a small development of houses adjoining the Coventry Road, one road away from Arthur Street. This was the first piece in the jigsaw, that would lead to the eventual formation of the Small Heath Alliance club. Young William Edden was destined to be a pivotal figure in it's rise, and one of the district's finest goalkeepers. At the age of two, he was the first of the club's founders to arrive in Small Heath. Not long afterwards, his mother gave birth to his two brothers; George in 1853 and Thomas in 1855. The three brothers would form the backbone of the Alliance football team for many years. Looking back, it seems almost incredible that George and Thomas were the only founders actually born in Small Heath. This in itself is an indicator of the wave of change that was about to engulf the area, something the three brothers would witness first hand.

When the Eddens first came to Small Heath it was still a relatively small settlement, growing around a busy tollgate on the main Coventry Road, positioned town-side of the junction with Green Lane. Their household was also town-side of the tollgate, blocked at one end by a huge railway embankment. For anyone travelling out of Birmingham through the tollgate, it was like entering a different world, escaping from the cramped and overcrowded dwellings that dominated the streets inside it. The well maintained turnpike road, once part of the main stagecoach route from London to Holyhead, had encouraged wealthy businessmen from Birmingham to build their country homes in what was rural Small Heath, away from the densely populated town centre. The convenience of the easy access to the town, and the rural feel of the area, made it popular with well to do businessmen and factory owners. Coventry Road was a sought after address, dominated by large detached residences in their own grounds, built on open meadows, and, importantly, benefiting from their own water pumps and stabling. One of the largest residences was Whitmore House a large Georgian building surrounded by several acres of estate. At least three Town Councillors lived on the road; Councillor John Suckling at Elmdon Villa, Councillor John Shakel at Blenheim House and Councillor John Lowe at Whitmore House.

Wealthy residents like these enjoyed a ready supply of clean water which they pumped up from underground springs. For the Eddens there was no such luxury. Like other town dwellers, they only had access to a shared well, and had no proper arrangements for dealing with raw sewage. It was a situation that was to have devastating consequences. In 1856, as winter set in, Sarah Edden, the boys' mother, was struck down with typhoid fever, a disease spread by insanitary conditions. Urgently she was consigned to a detached ward at Queen's Hospital, Birmingham, the place where infectious and contagious diseases were treated; but it was to no avail. Tired and emaciated following a fortnight of high fever and frequent delirium, she tragically passed away on 7th December 1856, at the age of only thirty seven. Nevertheless, in her three sons, she had left a strong legacy to the Alliance football club, making her, arguably, "the Mother of the Blues".

During the mid-Victorian era urban dwellers were in constant danger of contracting typhoid fever. In the countryside there didn't seem to be a problem, but in towns the growing concentration of people had a big impact on public health. Homes for ordinary working people lacked drainage, sewerage and running water. Routinely, excrement and urine was tipped onto soil heaps and cesspools near their homes which would invariably seep into the underground water supply, contaminating the wells. People just didn't understand that bacteria from the raw sewage caused diseases. Anyone who drank contaminated water or ate food which had come into contact with human faeces or urine was in danger. Bacteria could survive for weeks in the dried sewage piled up near houses. This could be spread around the muddy streets and trodden into the home. The Town Council did pay for the collection of human waste from outdoor privies and soil heaps at night-time, but this gave only temporary relief. Refuse and soil heaps continued to accumulate next to houses helping to swell the death rates of those living close by.

Queen's Hospital, where Sarah died, was a voluntary hospital relying on donations and subscriptions for its survival. It had been launched some fifteen years earlier by doctors seeking to aid medical research and most of the medical staff worked in honorary and unpaid posts. As a designated teaching hospital it was able to receive any unclaimed bodies for dissection and research. Sarah's admission would have been either through a subscriber's ticket, or a nomination by a hospital governor. Regular subscribers had the benefit of access to medical services at the site. There was no NHS. For working people the only alternative to a Queen's Hospital subscription ticket was to be treated in a workhouse "sick" ward alongside paupers' accommodation. Over 80% of hospital beds for the working classes were through the workhouse. The fact that Sarah received treatment in a voluntary hospital shows that the family had the foresight to subscribe, understanding the value of medical support. Today typhoid is easily treated using antibiotics, but in the 1850s these had not been developed. Even the rudimentary product of disinfectant, helpful in cleaning wards, did not evolve until the 1870s. It is notable that at least seven of the founding players suffered the tragic loss of at least one close family member during their early childhood.

One of the most prominent features of early Small Heath, half a mile from the Edden household, was the Small Heath Tavern, a large roadside hostelry dating back to the 1820s with stables and accommodation. Adjacent to the old tollgate, it attracted a mixed clientele, with regulars from all walks of life. There was even a patch of turf where parties of travelling gypsies were allowed to camp. Manual workers and tradesmen flocked to the pub to play various games, including "quoits", a popular outdoor game, where players threw metal rings at an iron peg in the ground, and "knock 'em down", a form of indoor skittles. The tavern's well established Bowling Green Club also made it a popular haunt for the wealthy and influential, with the bowling club's membership predominantly a mix of professional and well to do middle classes. These were men who could not only afford the club's annual subscription, which was ten shillings in 1851, but also had the free time to play games and dine afterwards. Even the cost of dinner, about two shillings, was beyond the means of ordinary working people. The wealthy clientele was also attracted by the close proximity of one of the town's premier cricket grounds, positioned behind the tavern on a wedge of land between the Coventry Road and Cattell Road.

Known as the Small Heath ground, it was arguably the town's top cricket venue. In 1851,1853 and 1854 an All England XI had played on the ground, and in 1855 and 1857 a United England XI appeared there, all in three day games. It features prominently in the history of Birmingham Cricket Club, with the club regularly holding its Annual General Meeting at the Small Heath Tavern throughout the 1850s and 60s. The standard of the playing surface was well regarded. A match report in the *Birmingham Daily Post* for the Birmingham versus Curdworth match in July 1860 reported that "a very good wicket was prepared, the ground being in beautiful order, as level as a billiard table." After the game a good dinner was supplied by Mr. Jones landlord of the Small Heath Tavern. With views across Birmingham from the ground and dining facilities at the tavern next door, it was a popular venue. The cricket matches here were probably the first experience the Edden brothers had of watching sport of any kind.

This idyllic setting would soon come under pressure from urban expansion, as building developments began encroaching on the ground in 1862. A brief note in the local press dated 3rd May 1862 stated that "in consequence of some alterations recently made near the Small Heath ground, it has been generally rumoured that the Birmingham Cricket Club has ceased to exist. Such, however, is not the fact. The formation of a new road near the ground has only taken away a small corner of the area hitherto used by the club - and the loss of that is scarcely apparent now that the fence has been readjusted." The Birmingham Cricket Club AGM took place at the Small Heath Tavern the following year in April 1863 as usual, but the long term future of the ground was under a definite threat.

In June 1863, a remarkable two day horse racing spectacle took place on ground at the rear of the tavern which attracted an amazing twelve thousand spectators on each day. Cleverly, the organisers had designed a three-quarters of a mile horse race, which ran across three adjoining pieces of land. The main part ran across the tavern's ground, but a portion also ran over Small Heath cricket ground, and a bordering field. Billed as the "Birmingham and Small Heath Races", it seems, in retrospect, to have been the last big sporting occasion on the land before houses encroached on the open space.

So what happened to Small Heath to rapidly change it from a semi-rural and sparsely populated settlement to an area of major urban development and industrial growth? The answer lay in the construction of a huge gun factory on a green field site in Small Heath, located between the GWR rail track and the Birmingham and Warwick Canal near to Golden Hillock Lane. A group of Birmingham gun makers had purchased the 25 acre site in 1861 and by the following year the manufacture of guns had begun. The factory, called Birmingham Small Arms (BSA), acted as a magnet for both new housing and people seeking employment. Within a year, GWR had built an additional station, Small Heath and Sparkbrook, to service the factory and the rapidly expanding population.

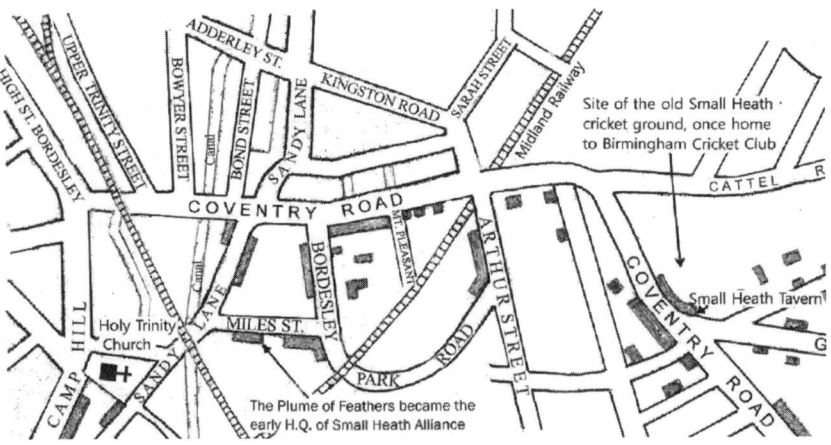

Small Heath c.1870, showing the streets around the Edden household in Mount Pleasant. To the west, the area adjoins Camp Hill, the location of Holy Trinity Church, and Bordesley High Street, the main route into the town centre via Deritend.

This was the beginning of Small Heath as a recognised residential area, and the catalyst for rows and rows of new terraced houses to be built on virgin land bordering

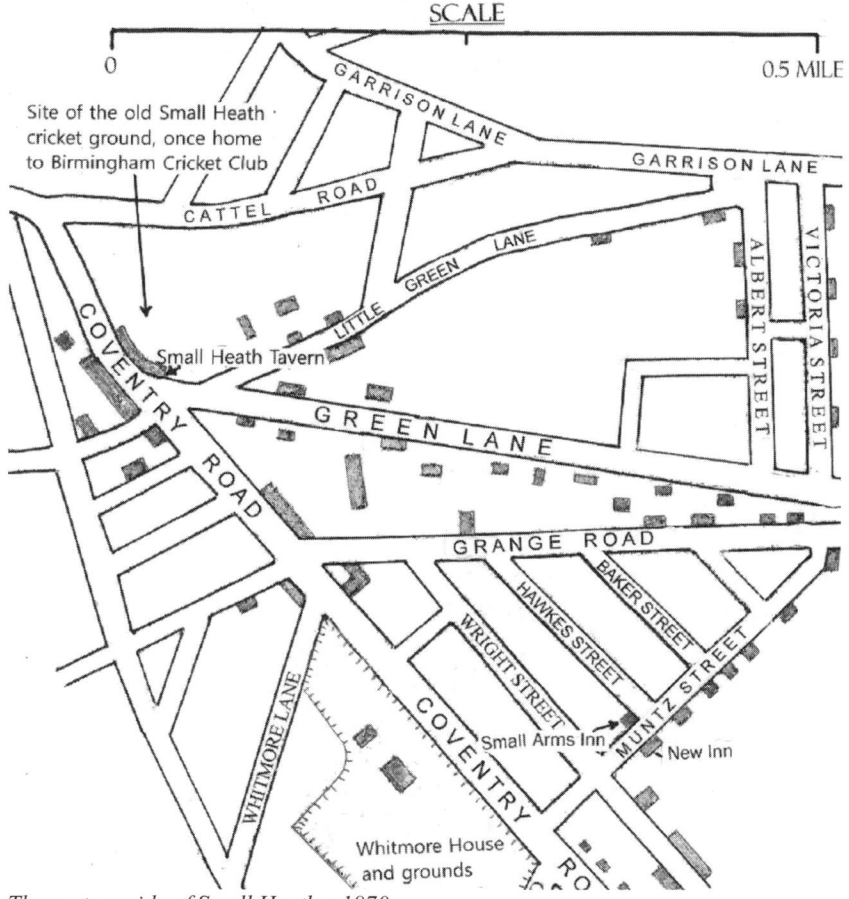

The eastern side of Small Heath c.1870.

the Coventry Road, away from the cramped and overcrowded courtyards of the town centre. These would soon overwhelm the more salubrious residences, completely changing the semi-rural feel of the area. During the 1860s workers and their families moved to the area in their droves attracted by jobs nearby and the new houses. This is the period when most of the founding players came to the area as children.

3
THE CRICKET CONVERTS

EXPLORING HOW ASSOCIATION FOOTBALL FIRST EMERGED IN BIRMINGHAM

For lads growing up in Small Heath during the 1860s, there was only one team sport which commanded mass appeal; cricket. The game completely dominated the sporting calendar. From late March to early October, any green open spaces or parkland became a natural focal point for young cricketers and their teams. Many teams in the vicinity struggled to find a suitable playing surface within Small Heath, and gravitated to the public pitches of Adderley Park, less than a mile to the north. One team who did find one, was the resourceful Small Heath Unity outfit. An advert placed in the *Birmingham Daily Gazette* (7th April 1866) led to them adopting a field at Little Green Lane in the heart of Small Heath.

The first evidence of any future Small Heath Alliance player taking part in a cricket match comes in 1867, when we find a seventeen year old Billy Edden, the Alliance's first goalkeeper, opening the batting for a team called Clifton, at Calthorpe Park, where his opponents were St. Martin's (*Birmingham Daily Gazette*, 11th September 1867). His team is thought to be linked to the Clifton Inn in Sparkbrook, and unconnected to the higher profile Aston Clifton club, which didn't come on the scene until around 1871. The Clifton Inn on Ladypool Lane had once been a farmhouse, an indication of the area's original rural setting. (Sadly the pub closed in August 2012). Trying to track young Billy's progress from pub cricketer to the Holy Trinity church team is a cheerless task. The earliest known fixture for the church team, under the name Trinity United, was a game at Aston Park on 22nd July 1865 against Percy, which was discovered listed in the *Birmingham Daily Post*. Frustratingly no player names are given.

It's seven years later before we get any further clues. Imagine the scene. It's a warm Saturday afternoon in the summer of 1872; the setting Adderley Park in the Saltley district of Birmingham. Trinity United are locked in a closely fought cricket match against Providence, which eventually sways in favour of the young Trinity team following a fine spell of bowling by twenty-two year old Billy Edden. For the players, the tranquil park surroundings were a welcome escape from the encroaching industrial landscape, and a rare opportunity to relax, away from the constant reminders of their usual daily grind. Above the tree line, smoke could be seen billowing from the chimneys of nearby factories. By far the biggest was the giant

Britannia Carriage Works enterprise, which stretched for thirteen acres between Arden Road and the London and North Western railway track, with over a hundred furnaces and forges on site. Inside the park boundaries, though, life was altogether more peaceful. This traditional cricket scene had remained largely unchanged at Adderley Park since it opened in 1857, as Birmingham's first council owned parkland. It was the place where several Alliance founders built their strong sporting ties.

In the Trinity United cricket team that day, Saturday 29th June 1872, were four key pioneers of the future Small Heath Alliance club; Billy Edden and his two younger brothers, Thomas and George, and one of the James brothers, most likely Tom. The full Trinity United team line-up was:
Shipton, Tedds, Hancocks, James, T. Edden, Meers, Upton, W. Edden, Fisher, Arrow and G. Edden. (source; *Birmingham Daily Post*, 4th July 1872).

The discovery of this team sheet is of great significance, as it not only provides the first known evidence of the early sporting links between the Edden and James families, but also confirms their connection to the Trinity Church team. In the previous summer (1871), three other members of the Trinity United team - Fisher, Hancocks and Upton - had been turning out for the local Camden Cricket Club, based at Calthorpe Park. Their opponents included Trafalgar (Aston), Oxford (a local team) and Clifton, Aston Park (not connected to Billy Edden's 1867 Clifton team). A year later, in 1872, the Clifton Aston Park cricket team included Matthews and Scattergood, two future founders of Aston Villa. There's no doubt that park cricket provided the game of football with an army of ready made team members, which enabled the new winter game to grow rapidly once it sprung up in the town.

At Adderley Park, it was the wide open spaces that acted as a magnet to dozens of cricket teams from the surrounding communities, including the Trinity Church lads. Small Heath Park didn't come into being until 1878, so it was Adderley Park where the local cricket enthusiasts gathered. Being a municipal park, the fields were free to use, and soon became a thriving focal point for the increasing numbers of representative teams being set up by the nearby pubs, churches and factories. Many of the factory teams were linked to the burgeoning railway industry, among them the Midland Locomotive, the London and North Western, and the Britannia Carriage Works clubs. The evidence that the Trinity United team was part of this sporting scene, places several key Alliance men near to the location where association football was first witnessed in Birmingham; Saltley College.

An ariel view showing the grounds of Saltley College. The square building at the top of the picture, surrounding a quadrangle, is the original extent of the college when it first opened in 1852, as the Worcester, Lichfield and Hereford Diocesan Training College. It was built in the style of an Oxford University college, with entry through a gateway at the porter's lodge.

In the early 1870s, at a time when the association game was hardly known in the Birmingham area, several of the college live-in students regularly played it, or at least their version, on the college playing fields. The young men at the Church of England college came from all parts of the country to train as teachers, usually for two years, and it was only natural for some to bring experience of the game from their home areas. Among the early football enthusiasts to study at the college were Tom Charles Slaney, the future captain and secretary of Stoke City F.C., and Frederick William Hackwood, the founder of the Wednesbury Town club, which in 1878 became the first in the district to enter the F.A. Cup.

It was 1871 when Tom Slaney first enrolled at Saltley College, already well-versed in the rules of association football after previously taking part in games near his home in the Penkhall area of Stoke. His mentor had been his teacher, John Thomas, the founder of Stoke Ramblers F.C. When the young Slaney started at Saltley College, fellow student Fred Hackwood was already in his second year, and the two soon became part of the vanguard of players who spear-headed the development of the game there. The College playing fields backed onto open meadows, making it easy for the local youths to watch these pioneering players develop their football skills and tactics. These sessions were ground breaking events. The play may have been unsophisticated, and undisciplined, with plenty of physical contact and rough play, but these were the first sightings of the modern game for most of the local residents, and the various cricket players who used Adderley Park as their base, just a stone's throw away from the college.

The college's Practising School, situated in an adjacent road, also helped to stoke up interest in the new winter sport. With nearly five hundred boys attending each day, the pupils acted as a natural coduit for telling others about it. It wasn't long before informal football games sprouted up at the municipal park, as local youths copied the college students. The thriving Adderley Park community was a natural channel for the sporting grapevine, with news of these exciting football developments gradually spreading through the streets and work places. In days before mass communication, word of mouth and local gossip was the prime source of information for any sports enthusiast.

At this stage cricket was still, by far, the most popular sport in the area and the only one attracting a regular student award at Saltley College. In line with tradition, the student cricket award was presented each November at the college's annual meeting. In 1872, there was a touch of irony, when the prize went to the football protagonist, Tom Slaney. As he picked up his cricket award, his mind was already on other things. During the autumn, several of his college pals had been sniffing out possible football opponents to challenge to a game. Were there any in the vicinity? Their quest must have been more in hope than expectation. Fortunately, an embryonic club called Incogniti was able to answer the call, and agree two fixtures. Also based in Saltley, it seems likely that the new team had derived their initial inspiration from the college lads. Their secretary, William Ingall, a seventeen year old commercial clerk, had recently moved with his parents to Hampden Cottage on Washwood Heath Road, Saltley, from nearby Duddeston. His father, George Ingall, was the Minister of Saltley Road Chapel, and an architect specialising in the design of chapels.

Not much is known about the first encounter between Incogniti and Saltley College, except that it finished in Incogniti's favour. In all likelihood, the match was played on the grounds of Saltley College, where the sports fields had a reputation for being corrugated and terribly uneven. In the return match, held at Adderley Park on 15th March 1873, Saltley College avenged their earlier defeat with a 3-0 victory. (source; *Birmingham Daily Post*, 19th March 1873). Early football publications were blissfully ignorant of these seminal games, and as a result they have remained unreported ever since. However, by disregarding the part played by the Saltley College students, and to a lesser extent the Incogniti club, early articles were effectively handing the credit for the introduction of modern football in Birmingham to two clubs outside of the Adderley Park epicentre; the Birmingham Clerks' Association Football Club in Edgbaston, and the Birmingham Cricket and Football Club in Aston.

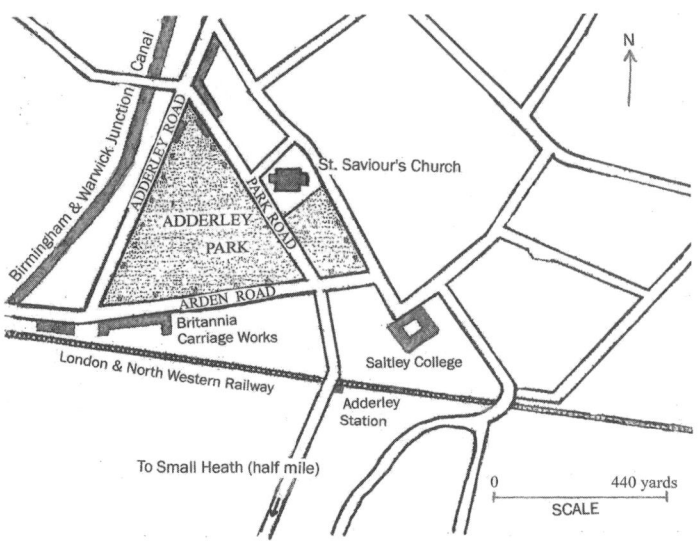

A map of Adderley Park in the early 1870s, showing it's close proximity to Saltley College. Two notable landmarks are the Britannia Carriage Works, which employed 900 men and turned out over 2,000 railway wagons and carriages each year, and St. Saviour's Church, whose football team was an early visitor to Small Heath Alliance's Ladypool Lane ground in 1876.

Even today, the accolade of Birmingham's oldest club is routinely given to the Birmingham Clerks' (later called Calthorpe F.C.), despite the creators, John Carson and John Campbell Orr, not even settling in Birmingham until October 1873, the season following the clashes between Saltley College and the Incogniti club. Part of the reason for this inaccuracy rests with Campbell Orr himself. In a letter published in Charles Alcock's 1876 *Football Annual*, Campbell Orr, by then secretary of the Birmingham and District F.A., wrote that "it was not until 1873 that association football made its appearance" (in Birmingham), and that "for one season the Calthorpe Club was the only Association Club." In other words he was placing himself as the founder of association football in Birmingham, and using his senior position within the local F.A. to promote the case. To be fair to Campbell Orr, as a newcomer to the town, it's possible that the previous season's events in Saltley had passed him by. On the other hand, as an avid football enthusiast, he was surely made aware of a letter printed in the *Birmingham Daily Post* on 15th November 1873, just a few weeks after his arrival, which said, "There is a club started last season, in the neighbourhood of Saltley, which plays association rules. The secretary's address is: Incogniti Football Club, Hampden Cottage, Washwood Heath Road".

Campbell Orr and Carson, both in their early twenties, had arrived in Birmingham to take up jobs as clerks, and soon struck up an enduring friendship, driven by their keen interest in sport. Both men came from well-to-do households in Scotland and benefited from having a good education. Campbell Orr attended St. Andrews University just a few miles east of where his father had been running his own printing factory in Cupar, Fife, with a work force of nearly thirty people. John Carson already had a football pedigree, having been an early pioneer of the Queens Park Football Club in Glasgow. After being brought up on a three hundred acres farm at Penningham, about twenty miles east of Stranraer, his family had moved to Maryhill in Glasgow during the late 1860s after the death of his father. Working in Glasgow as a clerk, he soon tagged on to a group of football playing clerks and businessmen from the offices and warehouses in the city who in 1867 had set up the ground breaking Queens Park club. With few other teams in existence, the young workers originally spent most of their time playing games against each other. It was during these hours of kick abouts that the Queens Park players developed an early passing game, described in early football terminology as "combination play". In one of their first games, a 14 aside match against Airdrie on 23rd June 1870, John Carson wrote himself into early football records by scoring one of the goals in a 4-0 victory. In the same year the Queens Park club joined the Football Association, favouring their rules, and even contributed a guinea towards the purchase of the original F.A. Cup.

Without Carson's involvement in the early Glasgow football scene, it is doubtful whether the Birmingham Clerks' club (later renamed Calthorpe) would have materialised. His unparalleled insight into association football tactics, such as team work and passing the ball, was something few early rival teams could match. Carson had a real passion for the game and as captain organised training and practice matches at their initial base, Calthorpe Fields, situated on the south-western edge of the town. Campbell Orr wrote, "this club (in 1873) had a severe struggle to keep members together, and we esteemed ourselves fortunate if on fine Saturdays we mustered 15 or 16 indifferent players"(source: 1876 *Football Annual*). He continued, "In the following season three or four new clubs sprang up, and for the first time Association matches were played here." No records exist of their first opponents, although my hunch is that one of their earliest were the Law Students from the university. Records show that two matches were played against them during the 1875-76 season, and I believe that these rather curious opponents were a legacy from the inaugural days of the club when mainstream opponents were in short supply. It is also easy to imagine the early practise sessions at Calthorpe Fields involving lads from the nearby King Edward VI Grammar school. The Clerks reputedly favoured the Football Association rules, as introduced by Carson following his spell in Glasgow.

On the opposite side of town in Aston, some other sporting developments were also taking place. It was almost by accident that early day sport entrepreneur and promoter Henry Quilter became involved in football. His primary sporting aim had only ever been to create the grandest cricket ground in Birmingham at the Lower Grounds, and attract the best players and teams to his venue. In 1873, at the age of forty-eight, he had spent £3,000, a sizeable sum at the time, on redeveloping his beloved cricket ground, without giving football a second thought. Football was not part of his plans, yet just twelve months later, almost under the radar, it arrived at the Lower Grounds as its popularity swept across the district. This episode demonstrates perfectly the speed at which football took hold from relative obscurity in 1873, when Quilter revamped his cricket ground, to mass appeal in just a matter of months.

The speed of its growth had taken Henry Quilter by surprise, even with his sporting connections. He had first become involved with Aston Lower Grounds in 1864, when it was nothing to write home about; just thirty-six acres of undistinguished meadowland. Previously during the 1850s, he had been the resident manager of Aston Hall and Park estate, a position he relinquished when it was purchased by Birmingham Corporation in 1864, the first historic country house nationally to pass into municipal ownership. It was then that he made his bold move to lease the adjacent Lower Ground meadows and develop them into a huge visitor attraction, with ornamental gardens, lakes and tearooms in one section, and a separate eight acre section reserved for sporting events. His aim was to get as many paying visitors through the gates as possible. Apart from investing heavily on landscaping the ornamental gardens, he also promoted sporting events, such as swimming galas and athletics meetings, which regularly attracted crowds of two to three thousand spectators. His main passion though was cricket. He arranged top class matches to draw in the crowds, regularly involving All England teams, and United South of England Elevens who included W. G. Grace on their team sheet. One stroke of luck for Quilter was that his initial investment in cricket at the Lower Grounds coincided with the gradual wane of the Small Heath cricket ground, as it fell victim to urban development. He would soon be able to entice the Birmingham Cricket Club away from their original Small Heath base.

As well as managing the Lower Grounds, Henry Quilter also ran the Holte Hotel in nearby Trinity Road. With all the events and activities a stones throw away, his hotel was always busy. His largest room could seat up to three hundred diners for sporting and business functions. The Birmingham Cricket Club, for example, regularly took dinner at the hotel. It was all excellent business for Quilter. The more popular the Lower Grounds became, the more business he generated for his hotel. His hotel was the original Holte Hotel, a three storey late Georgian house turned tavern which was eventually replaced in 1897 by the elegant Victorian building that still exists today.

His two sons, Charles and George, were keen cricketers having grown up watching matches at Aston Park since their childhood days. Both were born on the Aston Hall estate, Charles the eldest in 1856 and George two years later in 1858, and both would later work with their father managing the Lower Grounds' amenities. By the time the cricket ground was redeveloped in 1873, the two brothers were regulars in the

Birmingham Cricket Club team. Charles had been playing for the team since the age of fifteen. Reporting on the remodelled ground, the *Birmingham Daily Post* (10th April 1873) said, "All round the edge are planted young chestnut trees.........A broad carriage drive is carried round, flanked by deciduous shrubs, and these are backed up on two sides by rows of poplars. A pretty rustic refreshment room has been built at one end. Taking in the view of Aston Hall as part of the surroundings, it must be pronounced one of the prettiest cricket grounds in England."

Without doubt, Henry Quilter had achieved his aim of creating the top cricketing venue in Birmingham, impressing the members of the resident Birmingham Cricket Club. What he hadn't anticipated was that just over a year later he would be sharing the facilities with the sport of football. Football had simply not been on his horizon as he planned the cricket ground redevelopment, but he quickly realised that he needed to embrace the new trend. As the popularity of football gathered pace, it was a natural step for an existing cricket club to double up as a football club. He had the advantage of a readily available team made up of players from the cricket team, including his two sons, and wasted little time in setting up a prestigious football fixture at the Lower Grounds against the rival Birmingham Clerks' Association Football Club in the Autumn of 1874. Somewhat quirkily the home team named itself the Birmingham Cricket Football Club. Played on Saturday 21st November, the 13 a side game is the earliest local match I can find in the Birmingham press with a full match report and team line-ups, which certainly adds weight to the importance given to the fixture.

Unfortunately the spectacle was ruined by dense fog. The press report stated that "both teams played at great disadvantage, as it was impossible to see the ball at a distance of 20 yards in consequence of dense fog. The Birmingham Clerks' Association were several times at fault from not knowing the ground, and not seeing where the goal-posts were. Throughout the match, however, the ball was kept well in the quarters of the home team. For the Birmingham Cricket Club, Mr. Webster (captain) played an excellent half-back, and Messrs. Pears, Walker, Powell and Clarke did good service for their side; whilst Messrs. Carson (captain), Sutton, E. Blood and Orr distinguished themselves for the strangers."

Teams: Birmingham Cricket Football Club, Messrs. Webster (captain), Walker, Pears, Nicholls, Parry, Durkin, Powell, Clarke, Cofield, Young, Slack, George Quilter and C.H.Quilter

Birmingham Clerks' Association Football Club: Messrs. Carson (captain), Mason, Sutton, W. Blood, E. Blood, Orr, Lucas, Smart, Smalls, Glover, Crosby, Millarde and Virgo

The Lower Grounds did more than any other venue in Birmingham to bring football into the public's consciousness. With over 300,000 people visiting the Lower Grounds annually, it immediately helped to bring the game to the attention of the masses, giving first cricket and then football a shop window. Admittedly most visitors came to look at the ornamental gardens and stroll around the lakes, but many others took the opportunity to watch the sporting activities. For many it was their first taste of sport and they soon became hooked. There's no doubt that both the Birmingham Clerks' Club, and the Birmingham Cricket Football Club played a huge part in promoting the game in Birmingham, but the regular assertion that they were the two earliest clubs in the town, has meant that the key pioneering role played by Saltley College has been unfairly overshadowed.

Saltley College can also claim to have spread football to Wednesbury in the Black Country. After former student Frederick Hackwood had finished his teacher training, he returned to his hometown of Wednesbury, and duly set up the first association club there in 1873; Wednesbury F.C. Then, a year later, a second Wednesbury team followed his lead, when Wednesbury Old Athletic (originally known as The Wednesbury Literary and Athletic Institute) emerged.

A timeless cricket scene similar to those enjoyed by the Alliance founders during the 1860s and 70s, often at Calthorpe Park and Adderley Park. This photo shows cricket at Small Heath Park c.1900.

4
THE SMALL HEATH ALLIANCE CLUB IS UP AND RUNNING

The Small Heath Alliance club started life as a cricket club. It was during the spring of 1875 that several lads who played cricket for Trinity United, the Holy Trinity Church team, hatched their plan to set up their own club. It's generally accepted that a bulk of the club's initial team were regular attendees of the Holy Trinity Church, but the claim that several were choristers could be a romantic embellishment added later. The 1906 publication *Association Football and the men who made it*, merely states that the majority were "members of the congregation". Yet the chorister link still endures, perhaps fuelled by a change of team name to Trinity Choir, around the time the Alliance lads broke away from it. The constant rehearsals and practise needed, would have made the choir almost incompatible with any sporting ambitions. It was no place for part timers, being carefully choreographed and well drilled.

By the time of the club's formation the Small Heath area was well and truly on the map. Less than a year earlier, it had received a huge boost by being part of the Royal procession route for the visit of the Prince and Princess of Wales, the future King Edward VII and his wife Alexandra. On 3rd November 1874, the Royal procession had travelled down the Coventry Road, going past the streets where founders lived. Everywhere was draped in banners and decorations. The Small Heath Committee, established by local worthies to decorate the route, had erected a huge gothic arch near to the Greenway Arms, with four columns on each side of the road standing on a huge granite base. The whole population was in the streets occupying every vantage point, with sightseers packed onto every balcony and house roof as the procession passed through towards the town centre. The event had helped to give the locals a pride in the area and cement their sense of identity, something the founders were soon able to plug into.

The Small Heath Alliance club was following in the footsteps of two other cricket clubs who had previously used Small Heath in their name. Small Heath Unity was the first in the mid 1860s, followed by Small Heath Zingari in 1873. Small Heath Unity had sprung up not long after the Birmingham cricket club, the most prominent in the district, had left the waning Small Heath ground to take up residence at Quilter's Lower Grounds in 1864. Small Heath Zingari was named in homage to a nationally renowned cricket club called I Zingari, a wandering team of amateurs founded in 1845 by a group of public school boys whose aim had been to nurture amateur cricket to combat the rising tide of professionalism.

Both the Unity and Zingari clubs were the domain of the well to do and aspiring middle classes. The Unity team included John M. Lowe from the grand Whitmore House residence on Coventry Road, where his father, John Lowe senior, a prominent local councillor, employed three servants. Other team mates included a barrack master's son, and sons of two local factory owners. Their relative wealth meant that their club could even afford to engage two cricket professionals. The new Alliance club, on the other hand, had no such standing. It was an ordinary grassroots club, not bothered about social status, and this meant that it could connect with the ordinary working people. With the area now home to a huge influx of cosmopolitan tradesmen and factory workers, the club was immediately in tune with the changing face, and new found pride in the area.

The first known Alliance match was played at Calthorpe Park on 31st July 1875, against St. Andrew's, also from Small Heath. The Alliance team included a trio of surnames from the known Trinity United cricket eleven from 1872 (Arrow, Edden and James), and it's probable that several other team members also had past links to the church team. In an enthralling game, the Alliance won by just one run, with bowler Tom James taking a hat-trick of victims to force an amazing victory. (*Birmingham Daily Post*, 3rd August 1875). The full Alliance line-up was:

Billington, T. James, Edden, A. James, Edmonds, Barr, Teychennie(sic), Insall, Arrow, Barmore, Quarton.

This newly discovered team sheet indicates that the ex-Trinity Church cricketers had simply formed another cricket club, and it's likely that plans to continue with a winter football section were only triggered a few months later. It also confirms that Arthur James was part of the Alliance set up from the outset. This is significant, as many modern accounts have previously assumed that his first playing involvement wasn't until the opening game of the 1876/77 football season, against Wednesbury Old Park. The truth is that Arthur James was with the Alliance club right from the beginning, although there remains a continuing uncertainty about his first football appearance. We know for sure that he didn't play in the first game against Holte Wanderers, but as the make up of any other Alliance teams for 1875/76 is unknown, we can't be certain that he didn't take part later that same season. It is generally regarded, however, that his football debut was on 7th October 1876, the opening match played at Ladypool Lane.

The three James brothers, Thomas, Arthur and Fred, lived in Cattell Road, the same street as another prominent player, Billy Edmonds. It was a bustling and crowded household, with four sisters and five brothers in total. Tom and Arthur both followed their father into the industrial fender fitting trade, whereas younger brother Fred, who had initially worked as an errand boy from the age of twelve, finally settled into a job as a rule maker.

Billy Edmonds

The home of Billy Edmonds was much quieter, shared only with his widowed step-grandmother. His grandfather, who had given the orphaned Billy a home, had died in 1867. Billy worked as an articled clerk in an accountants office, a completely different working environment to the James brothers. Yet despite his middle-class occupation, he was just one of the gang, raised in the same streets, and sharing a love of sport.

Their pals, Billy, Tom and George Edden at Mount Pleasant, were just a short stroll away on the route towards Holy Trinity Church. The Church was a major hub of the community, placed between the older crowded area of Deritend and the fast expanding neighbourhood of Small Heath stretching eastwards away from the town centre. It had a large following with crowds of 400 to 500 attending Sunday morning Holy Communion, and evensong with sermons regularly attracting 700 to 800 parishioners. It's easy to imagine all the lads discussing their plans for their own cricket club as they mingled after church and made their way home together up Camp Hill and onto the Coventry Road. By the Autumn of 1875, they had also decided to add a football section to keep themselves occupied throughout the winter months. At this time, the local football scene was in a fairly confused state, with two differing codes of Association rules being played across the area.

The competing versions were Sheffield rules, championed by the well established Sheffield Association, with strongholds throughout Yorkshire, the East Midlands and

Staffordshire, and the London based Football Association version which had been created in an effort to establish a single national code. During the mid-1870s, the town of Birmingham was a kind of melting pot for both versions, although it is fair to say that the Sheffield version was gaining the upper hand. It was favoured by the esteemed Birmingham Cricket Football club (not linked to the modern Birmingham City F.C.) based at Aston Lower Grounds, and through their influence it became the dominant version across the district.

None the less, with large numbers of new and inexperienced teams springing up all the time, games in Birmingham and the surrounding districts remained a real hotchpotch. Even amongst the more established teams, there was a lack of consistency on the number of players allowed in each team. For instance, when the Birmingham Cricket Football Club played the Birmingham Clerks' Association Football Club in November 1874, there were thirteen players per side. While in the Black Country, fifteen a side games were common. Different again, a representative game between the Sheffield Association and Birmingham, in November 1875, was a twelve a side affair. It was played at the home of Sheffield rules football, Bramhall Lane, and in the following month, the newly formed Birmingham and District Football Association gave it's support to adopting the Sheffield rules version of the game across the whole Birmingham district. At last the district had some direction and clarity, but at a cost. The choice of Sheffield Rules was at odds with the prestigious F.A. Cup competition, and hindered local teams from competing in it, an inconvenience which was to continue for two seasons; 1875/6 and 1876/77. This was the confused and fairly disjointed Birmingham football scene that the Small Heath Alliance men were part of in 1875.

Little is known about their inaugural football season. Indeed, there is a frustrating lack of information on the Small Heath Alliance club in general, something that William McGregor, the Villa vice-President and founder of the Football League, was all too ready to point out. In a 1906 article published in *The Book of Football* (edited by C. F. Alcock and F. J. Wall), he remarked that the Alliance's history was "not so fully recorded in minute books" as the history of his own club. Ironically, it now seems likely that this article on the Small Heath club, is the earliest surviving source of their first ever team sheet, and without William McGregor's passion for writing about football, such details might have been lost. He listed the team for their first organised football fixture, versus Holte Wanderers, as follows:
W. Edden, Arthur Wright, Fred James, Tom James, G. H. Edden, W. H. Edmunds[sic] (captain), T. Edden, D. Keys, C. Barmore, C. Barr and J. Sparrow.

Notice that he misspells Billy Edmonds' surname as Edmunds, which helps to explain why it is commonly written that way today. Importantly, McGregor's list confirms that Billy Edmonds was the first football captain of the club. Decades later in 1989, author Tony Matthews made the claim in his *Complete Record* publication, that there were twelve members in the inaugural line up and gives the name of the 'missing' player as Richard Morris. Unfortunately he gives no source for this information. If the game was played to Sheffield rules, it makes sense that a team of twelve could have taken the field. It seems odd, though, that McGregor would omit one of the players from his teamsheet. Trying to trace the possible identity of Richard Morris (e.g. date of birth, address and occupation) has not proved possible. For the eleven players listed in McGregor's article, a brief pen picture of their early lives is given below, together with their addresses as taken from the 1871 census records (the nearest year available). The addresses give a clear indication of their close proximity to each other. The details are:

Charles Richmond Barmore.... Birch Terrace, Grange Road.

Charles Barmore arrived from the Black Country as a young child, when his father was drawn to the area by the pull of the new B.S.A. gun factory. His father was originally part of the traditional cottage industry in his native Darlaston, where gun components were made at home based workshops. Although he made a good living, he was often left uncertain on the amount of work he would be given. Increasingly the work was given to larger mechanised factories, where the orders could be turned out much quicker and more cheaply than by outworkers in small scale workshops. The writing was on the wall for Darlaston's declining gun trade, and Charle's father knew that he needed to make the move to nearby Birmingham to improve his prospects. It wasn't long before the family gravitated to Small Heath and the newly opened B.S.A. Factory.

Charles John Barr............94, Kyrwick's Lane.

Charles "Chas" Barr was born in Dean Street, near to the Bull Ring market, where his father ran a draper's business. His dad had started working life in Coventry, as one of eight "live in" draper's assistants. When conditions in the Coventry cloth industry started to deteriorate, he moved the short distance to Birmingham, to set up his own drapers and milliners business, which thrived. Not only did he employ an assistant and an apprentice, he was also able to take on two servants just like his old draper master in Coventry.

George Henry Edden
Thomas White Edden
William "Billy" Edden..........9, Mount Pleasant.

Their father, Thomas, a bricklayer from Alveston near Stratford-upon-Avon moved to Birmingham in the late 1840s with his new wife Sarah. William Edden (the club's first goalkeeper), their first son, was born on 11th February 1850 at 57 Rea Street in Digbeth. Within a couple of years the family had moved across the river Rea to the newly built street of Mount Pleasant in Small Heath, a small cul-de-sac of around twenty five houses just off the Coventry Road. Here Sarah gave birth to two more founding players, George Henry Edden in 1853 and Thomas White Edden in 1855. Mount Pleasant was one of Small Heath's earliest housing developments prior to the massive expansion of the 1860s. Moving to the area before the housing boom was either a shrewd move or just a lucky decision by their father. Either way, as a builder, he had plenty of work as his family grew in size. Sadly, the boys' mother, Sarah, died in 1856 after a bout of typhoid.

William "Billy" Henry Edmonds……30, Cattell Road.

The childhood of the club's first captain, Billy Edmonds was also blighted by family tragedy. When he was just a year old, his father, Robert Bruce Edmonds, a merchants clerk, died of blood poisoning. By the age of nine, he had also lost his mother, Eliza Warren Edmonds (nee Smith). Fortunately he was surrounded by a strong family network. The Edmonds family had run the nearby Hope and Anchor Inn in Navigation Street since the early 1800s, and his grandfather, Robert Edmonds, was now the landlord. A lively and well frequented pub, it was well known for its music nights and political debates in the large rooms at the rear of the building. The town centre pub was at the heart of the community and well tuned to the popular politics of the day. Public houses were places where many working men heard about local news and learned about current issues. With no radios or televisions and a sizable minority not able to read, newspapers and periodicals were often publicly read aloud stimulating debates and discussions. Like many urban pubs, the Hope and Anchor was a hub for those demanding wider voting rights. Working men reasoned that if they had the vote, they could have more say in their working and living conditions. Rooms at the pub were regularly used by local campaigners and politicians to address packed meetings of tradesmen and artisans, who demanded the right to vote, and some concessions were eventually gained in 1867.

It was the death of his mother in 1863, that brought the eight year old Billy Edmonds to Small Heath. He was taken in by his maternal grandfather, David Smith, a Scottish born engineer who had recently retired after twenty years as manager of the Fazeley Street Gasworks, where he had lived on-site. On retirement he had chosen a house in Cattell Road to set up home with his second wife Eliza, twenty years his junior, and Billy Edmonds, his orphaned grandson. As if by fate, Billy was now in the same street where the James family would eventually settle, including brothers Tom, Arthur and Fred.

Frederick William James
Thomas James……165, Cattell Road (also included Arthur James).

The James family was also part of this surge in workers migrating to the area in 1862. Players Tom, Fred and Arthur James were born in Rotherham, all making the trek south as young children when their father Mark James came to Birmingham in search of a better job. In Rotherham, the family had rented a small property in the yard of Wellgate House, but on the death of their old landlord, the family had been forced to move out by the new owners. It was a difficult time for the family, especially with five children all under the age of eight. Thomas was the eldest son, aged seven, followed by Arthur, five and Fred, just three years old. Their father worked as a stove grate fitter. In the 1860s Rotherham had been a major centre for the stove grate industry with several iron foundries specialising in stove grate and fender manufacture. However competition for fitting work was tough and Mark had been supplementing his income with occasional farming work and taking in a boarder at his home just to get by. With no prospects, he decided to take the plunge and move his family to Birmingham, where he soon found work as an industrial fender fitter. By 1865, the family had settled in Cattell Road, in the heart of Small Heath, after first living in nearby Watery Lane.

David Keys……….130, Moseley Road.

The last of the founding players to arrive in the Small Heath area was David Keys, a lone teenager who came to take up a job as a telegraph clerk around 1870, some five years before the first match. It must have been a daunting prospect to be starting a new job in unfamiliar surroundings. Sixteen year old David Keys had spent most of his childhood living in family quarters at the Royal Artillery Barracks in Greenwich, the headquarters of his father's artillery brigade. He was now moving into the unknown, changing the ordered and protective environment of army quarters to the hustle and bustle of life in Small Heath. He must have had mixed emotions about the move, with feelings of apprehension softened by his sense of adventure and new found freedom. With no family in Birmingham, he initially stayed in lodgings at 130 Moseley Road, just a few hundred yards from Trinity Church. He probably felt, at least initially, a bit of an outsider, but he would soon find that Small Heath was a cosmopolitan and vibrant area attracting workers and their families from all over the United Kingdom. He quickly made friends, amongst them a group of sports enthusiasts who played cricket for Trinity Church.

Samuel Joseph "Joe" Sparrow………175, Bordesley Park Road.

From the age of eleven, Joe Sparrow was orphaned and brought up in Small Heath by his uncle, following the demise of both his father, an engine fitter from Bordesley, and mother. His uncle, Joseph Sparrow senior, worked as a bone and ivory turner, making hat pins and cutlery handles, using a foot pedal lathe, probably in a small workshop attached to his Small Heath home. Young Joe soon picked up his uncle's turning skills, and followed him into the trade, creating ornaments and utensils from animal bones. The work was low paid and the working conditions surprisingly hazardous. A fine dust would drift around the workshop from the carved bones, and build up in the lungs of the workers. A respiratory hazard known as "pneumoconioses", bone workers lung, was a common ailment. The awful stench of drying animal bones, usually horse, also contributed to the unglamorous conditions.

Arthur Henry Wright….29, Muntz Street (next door to the New Inn).

His father, James, had progressed into the gun trade after many years of home working as an unskilled metal worker, initially toiling as a snaffle maker (metal rings for horse bridles) in a small work shop at the back of his Walsall home in Blue Lane. Arthur's father would sit and make scores of these each day, cutting lengths of thin metal strips and hammering them into shape on an anvil. This kind of repetitive task was typical of many Black Country outworkers who tended to undertake a range of fairly rudimentary tasks, such as nail and chain making. The more highly skilled work remained in nearby Birmingham and this is where Arthur's father soon settled. After a spell as a sword cutter, a trade in decline, he transferred his outworker skills to supplying components for the growing gun trade. By 1871 the Wright family, including fourteen year old Arthur, had moved to Muntz Street in the heart of Small Heath. His father was now making gun parts, no doubt to help fill the demand created by the huge BSA gun factory a few streets away.

At the time of the 1871 census, only one of the football founders was still at school; fourteen year old Arthur Wright. He was a talented artist, and it's believed that he later progressed to Birmingham School of Art, going on to become a lithographic artist. The others, in order of age, were employed as follows:
Fred James, age 12, errand boy.
Charles Barmore, age 13, B.S.A. factory worker.
Chas Barr, age 13, junior clerk.
Joe Sparrow, age 14, machinist (bone worker).
Thomas Edden, age 15, labourer, probably building.
Billy Edmonds, age 16, accountant's articled clerk.
Thomas James, age 16, fender fitter (Arthur James, age 14 was also a fender fitter).
David Keys, age17, telegraph clerk.
George Edden, age 17, bricklayer.
Billy Edden, age 21, bricklayer.

The young men who founded the Alliance club were dedicated sports enthusiasts. They needed to be. There was no glamour involved, and no payments. For five and a half days each week they toiled in their day jobs, using what little free time they had to organise their team activities and training sessions. Their club had no funds and no assets, it's only income being the lowly subscriptions paid by each player. When the football section was unfolded, the players had insufficient funds to even rent a field. Ever resourceful, they used their local knowledge to identify a patch of disused wasteland in Arthur Street, just off the Coventry Road, to use as their first playing base. It's in these unpretentious surroundings that their football endeavours began.

The budding footballers had the time between the end of the cricket season in late September, and their first football fixture in November, to get "into condition". During the fast fading light of the Autumn evenings practice games were not feasible. Realistically, only keep fit exercises, together with jogging and sprinting routines, and the occasional longer distance run could be undertaken. Actual football practice using a ball was limited to Saturday afternoons, the only regular opportunity the players had for gathering in sufficient daylight. This seemed to be the norm for the time. When Coventry Wanderers Football Club was established in January 1875, just ten miles from Small Heath, the *Coventry Herald* newspaper reported that their players met up every Saturday afternoon at their field near Quinton, which they used as a practice ground. Apparently they chose to play association rules as it was considered "more scientific and less dangerous than rugby union."

It's unlikely that a fledging club like the Alliance had a plentiful supply of footballs, due to their relatively high cost. As late as November 1884, a replacement ball was not available during an important Birmingham Cup tie at Muntz Street, after the original one had burst, leaving the game against Excelsior to end in an abrupt fashion. This suggests that in early training sessions only a single ball was available, automatically limiting the opportunities for individual players to hone their skills and ball control. Traditionally leather football cases were cut out and sewn together by the local shoemaker, but as association football gained popularity amongst the working and artisan classes, they became cheaper as larger scale manufacturers started to turn them out.

There was no standard kit for the Alliance men, only what each player could adapt from his day to day clothing. In many working class households, family members had only one change of clothes available, so using clothing for football might have required some hard choices. Players were limited to what they had available, some using woollen type garments and others cotton vests. It is thought that the earliest Alliance colours were nearer to navy blue than the royal blue used in modern day strips, with each player's shirt inevitably a slightly different shade of dark blue, due to the random nature of the clothing used and the fact that most shirts were dyed at home. These were frugal times, when clothing was purchased only when needed, so kits were frequently patched and mended to keep them going.

The oldest player in the team was twenty-five year old William "Billy" Edden, the goalkeeper. Goalkeeping was a tough job, with the laws of the game offering little protection. Opposition forwards were free to charge at keepers even if the ball was nowhere near, deliberately clattering into them and roughing them up with impunity. To withstand this barrage of assaults, keepers needed to be physically strong, and able to stand up to frequent bruising knocks and winding blows, without being intimidated. Billy Edden had all of these qualities. Working as a bricklayer in all weathers, he was as tough as they come and as strong as an ox. His arms and wrists were naturally strengthened by his building work, honed by the constant handling of weighty bricks, enabling him to brush aside challenges with his brute strength. His nickname of 'Pouncer' also suggests a fair amount of agility, and a knack of diving through the crowded goalmouth to claim the ball.

The average age of the outfield players was just under nineteen years, with five teenagers in the side. The five were Chas Barr, Joseph Sparrow and Arthur Wright, all eighteen, and Charlie Barmore and Fred James, both seventeen. Fred James was the youngest, only turning seventeen a few weeks earlier. The youthful make up of the team indicates that it was a young man's game. After the daily grind of work, it was clear that only the younger men still had energy to burn. Nine of the players were also free of domestic responsibilities, still living at home with their parents, or in the case of Billy Edmonds his step-grandmother. Only Billy Edden and Tom James were married.

The likelihood is that only a handful of games were played by the Alliance during their first season, all low key events and raising no more than a flicker of interest among local residents. Interestingly, I found a single fixture advertised in the local press, a return match against Holte at Aston Park on 25th March 1876, a week before the start of the new cricket season. The result is unknown.

The accolade of scoring the Alliance's first goal went to twenty-one year old telegraph clerk David Keys. The goal, in the 1-1 draw with Holte Wanderers, gave him an indelible place in the club's history. Most footballers can only dream of this kind of achievement, but for David Keys it seemed just typical of his exploits. Much of his life reads like an epic adventure from a Victorian boys' own magazine, full of both triumph and misfortune, with football almost the least extraordinary episode of his colourful life. A talented athlete, he prided himself on keeping in prime condition. Like many early footballers, it was his running ability and physical fitness which caught the eye, rather than his skill with the ball. He had already built up a reputation as one of the most accomplished runners in the district, and getting him into the team was a smart move. A year earlier, in October 1874, he had totally dominated a sports event organised by the Small Heath Zingari cricket club, on grounds at the rear of the Sydenham Hotel. His versatility was impressive, rewarded with the champion's prize of a gold centred medal. He won races across four distances from 100 yards to one mile, including the 120 yards hurdles. His links with the Alliance club only lasted a couple of seasons due to a dramatic turn of events which eventually took him away from Small Heath.

Amazingly his life had begun in the Scottish Highlands. It was in the small harbour village of Fortrose on the Black Isle where his mother, Matilda Keys, gave birth to him in April 1854. Overlooking the Moray Firth, the isolated community of Fortrose was difficult to reach by road and had no rail connection. In fact most trade and visitors came by sea. The tidal harbour, built by Thomas Telford in 1817, was the main focus of the village with a daily steamer service to Inverness, a journey of ten miles along the Moray Firth. As it happens, their son's birth in Scotland was purely an accident of history. Both David's parents, Matilda and George Keys, were born in Ireland. So why were they here?

The answer lay a short trip across the Moray Firth at Fort George. It was here, at the most impressive artillery fortification in Britain, that David's father, a gunner in the Royal Artillery, was on a military detachment from his Woolwich base. The huge Fort George structure enclosed an area of forty two acres and housed more than 1,600 infantry soldiers from the Highland Regiments plus a small detachment of gunners from Woolwich. It was originally built to deter further Jacobean unrest in Scotland following the defeat of Bonnie Prince Charles at Culloden in 1746. The fort, however, was never called upon in anger and was kept purely as an infantry garrison. Life at the fort for Gunner Keys would have been fairly uneventful, interrupted only by routine firing drills for the muzzle-loaded heavy artillery guns. He had originally joined the British Army in 1842 in his home town of Armagh in Ireland at the age of 18. After a few years of serving as a foot soldier, he transferred to the Royal Artillery as a gunner.

The 1861 census shows eight year old David Keys living at Woolwich barracks with his parents alongside other military families. The young David Keys spent much of his early life in military quarters with his mother Matilda, often while his father was away for several months at a time as part of British expeditionary forces abroad. In 1861, Royal Artillery Field Batteries from Woolwich were sent to both New Zealand and Canada. David's father was eventually discharged via Chelsea hospital due to injury in the 1870s, with a useful army pension.

The army exploits of his father seem to have had a big impact on David's approach to life, particularly in his inclination to take risks. One of his more notable gambles occurred around 1877 in Small Heath, when he decided to leave the relative security of his telegraph clerk job to set up a bedding manufacturing business with his nineteen year old friend and club mate, Jean Benjamin Teychenne. The whole venture seemed shaky from the outset. For a start, David Keys was a complete novice to manufacturing and the world of business. At least his co-partner Teychenne, who lived on the Coventry Road with his parents and eleven siblings, had previously gained some practical experience in the trade. He had been apprenticed locally to his French born father, who specialised in chemically purifying feathers so that they could be used in mattresses, but this hardly qualified him to run a business. For the two ambitious entrepreneurs, however, there were no such doubts. Buoyed by the kudos of being their own bosses, they proudly traded under the name "Teychenne and Keys", operating from their Phoenix Works in Glover Street.

At the same time, David Keys still found time to pursue his passion for sport, continuing to take part in local athletics events like the one held at the Aston Lower Grounds on 2nd June 1877, organised by the Birmingham Cricket Club. Keys ran in the two miles race, while his Alliance team mates, Billy and George Edden, both lined up in the one mile walking race. Keys, now living in Garrison Lane Small Heath, must have felt that his life was on a roll, enjoying both the cut and thrust of business life and the comradeship of his friends from the Alliance club. What's more, he had become romantically involved with one of his business partner's sisters, seventeen year old Eleonore Teychenne, and on 22nd July 1878 they were married at the local St. Peters and St. Pauls Church.

Unfortunately, just over three months later, the "Teychenne and Keys" business venture collapsed with debts of around £500, a large sum for the time. It was a shocking reversal of fortune for both men, who were now penniless and being chased by creditors. With their reputation in tatters, an agreement was reached with the receivers to pay the creditors just seven shillings in the pound.

The ordeal seems to have had a profound impact on David Keys. With the unravelling of his business, he made the bold decision to start a new life with his wife on the other side of the world in New Zealand. It wasn't a journey for the feint hearted. Voyages typically took around ninety two days, passing the Cape of Good Hope on the southern tip of South Africa and journeying across the vast Pacific Ocean. Until 1880, the British Government was actively encouraging the migration of British settlers to the far-off colony by offering travellers free passage, a tempting factor for a young couple in severe financial straits. This gave David Keys the chance to start afresh and rebuild his life. In New Zealand he was able to go back to his original line of work, as a telegrapher. The telegraph service in the southern hemisphere was still in it's infancy. An undersea cable had only reached New Zealand in 1876 when it was laid on the sea floor from Botany Bay near Sydney in Australia. Once connected, for the first time New Zealand was in direct communication not only with Australia, but also Asia, Europe and the United Kingdom. David Keys was an early pioneer of the New Zealand telegraph service, first working in the town of Napier, on the North Island at Hawke Bay, starting his job on 23rd August 1879, and then following the service to the South Island as it expanded, eventually settling in Dunedin where he spent the rest of his life.

A copy of David Keys' employment card covering the period 1893 to 1910. It was found in the New Zealand National Archives in Wellington, NZ. He originally joined the NZ Telegraph Service in August 1879. Sadly he died within two weeks of his retirement, on 2nd March 1910 in Dannevirke, NZ, suffering from stomach cancer. He was 53.

5
THE BIRTH OF THE BIRMINGHAM & DISTRICT FOOTBALL ASSOCIATION AND IT'S POWER STRUGGLE WITH THE ASTON LOWER GROUNDS COMPANY

The Birmingham and District Football Association was set up on 8th December 1875, several months after the Alliance club's formation, following a series of events triggered by Henry Haywood Webster, a Sheffield metal smith. He was the captain of the Birmingham Cricket and Football Club, and arguably one of the most significant contributors to the development of the early football landscape in Birmingham. It was his strong links with the thriving Sheffield football scene, and their local F.A., that eventually led to the creation of a copycat ruling body in Birmingham. Yet Webster's role has, until now, remained hidden and never given the recognition that it deserves. Little did he know when he organised the ground breaking home and away games for Birmingham Cricket and Football Club, against the renowned Sheffield Football Association team, that it would have such a significant impact on football in Birmingham. By giving local players and the watching public the chance to see the top Sheffield footballers of the day, considered amongst the best in the country, Webster would inspire the Birmingham football community to be more ambitious.

The road towards a Birmingham Football Association all started when the twenty-eight year old Webster moved down from Sheffield in 1874, and was immediately given the captaincy of the Birmingham Cricket Club. Considering that the club attracted mainly well-to-do young men in middle class jobs, at first glance this seems a little odd. My belief is that he was specially recruited by Henry Quilter, proprietor of the Lower Grounds, to be the club's cricket professional and coach. In his native Yorkshire Webster had already built a reputation as a talented cricketer, regularly turning out for the Wednesday Cricket Club and twice selected to play for Yorkshire, against Middlesex and Surrey, in 1868. Quilter had been looking to boost the quality of his team following his heavy investment in the ground, and Webster was his man. In the summer before his appointment Webster had been in fine form for the Hallamshire Wanderers Cricket Club in Sheffield, and once in Birmingham, his play soon caught the eye again. *The Birmingham Daily Post* described his innings of 63 against Derby on 31st August 1874 as "one of the finest displays of cricket ever witnessed at the Lower Grounds." The press reports in his native Sheffield were also glowing. *The Sheffield Independent* reported that the "feature of the Birmingham total was the batting of H. H. Webster, a Sheffielder, and one of the most promising batting colts the county of York ever tried, but for some reason relinquished." By the following summer, in June 1875, Webster was representing the Birmingham and

District Cricket team at Lords in a match against the M.C.C., whose team included W. G. Grace in their ranks. Inevitably W. G. Grace took five wickets, including the wicket of H. H. Webster.

Having been engaged by Henry Quilter to boost the profile of his cricket club, it is ironic that Webster's biggest impact came on the football side. Following his highly successful first cricket season at Lower Grounds, he soon became a central figure in the emergence of the Birmingham Football Club as one of the pre-eminent in the town. As luck would have it, in Sheffield, he had previously been part of the Wednesday Cricket Club at the time it added a football section in 1867. Described in the *Sheffield Telegraph* (22/11/1875) as a "much above average football player" and "an able coach", Webster had experienced at first hand the developing football talents at the Wednesday Club, which included Charles Clegg, a player who went on to play for England in the first ever football international, against Scotland in 1872.

At the Lower Grounds he began to pass on his tactical know-how, and not least his expertise of the Sheffield rules version of the game. The match report for their initial encounter with the Sheffield Association at Bramhall Lane, observed that the Birmingham team at first "held their own, and showed a knowledge of the Sheffield rules which surprised the spectators, who, as a rule, expected to find them raw hands...." (*Birmingham Daily Post*, 22/11/1875). This was due to Webster's expert schooling and coaching, although in football terms the team were still in their infancy. *The Sheffield Telegraph* commented that the Birmingham team "have yet to learn the great secret of success in football - viz., playing in their places. It is this equal division of labour in football, as in pin-making or any other business, that saves much waste of energy." The Sheffield team contained an array of stars. Apart from Charles Clegg, there were three other England men, his brother William Edwin Clegg, Billy Mosforth and Jack Hunter.

The initial two games were charity matches played in support of the Sheffield Football Players' Accident Society. On the day after Boxing Day 1875, the Sheffield men brought their crack team to Aston Lower Grounds. This was a big scoop for Webster, arranging for the strongest Association team to play in Birmingham. Even though his Birmingham team lost 4-0, after previously losing 6-0 in Sheffield, the crowd had been treated to a fine display of football. It was the first time that the Lower Grounds had witnessed such a flowing demonstration of organised teamwork mixed with skilful individual play. The two matches had proved a real boon to football in Birmingham, as local teams now set their sights higher. What's more Webster had arranged for the fixture to be repeated in the following season, 1876/77.

The Birmingham F.C. team for their inaugural game against the Sheffield Football Association, a 12 a side affair on 20th November 1875, was:

H.H. Webster (captain), G. Pears, F. Bill, J. Campbell Orr, J. Carson, W.J. Nicholls, F. Barnes, W. Handy, J. Cartwright, J.T. Eldridge, G.R. Quilter and J.H. Cofield.

Interestingly the team included the two most prominent players from the Birmingham Clerks' team (later to be called Calthorpe), who had played against the Birmingham Cricket F.C. team, led by Webster in November 1874. The two players, Scotsmen John Campbell Orr and John Carson, now lined up alongside their previous opponents from Birmingham F.C. *The Birmingham Daily Post* called it a team "chosen from clubs in Birmingham", but it wasn't an official team from the Birmingham and District Football Association. That hadn't been formed yet and it is doubtful whether a local Association would have even been on the horizon had it not been for Webster's initiative to organise games against the Sheffield F.A. The game at Bramall Lane seems to have been a catalyst for the football enthusiasts in Birmingham to spring into action and set up their own Association, with the Calthorpe duo, John Campbell Orr and John Carson, at the forefront. Inspired by what they had observed in Sheffield, they immediately set about replicating the arrangements in Birmingham. The well organised Sheffield Association had impressed them both, and at the post-match dinner held at the Aldelphi Hotel, they used the opportunity to find out how it worked and how it benefited football in Sheffield.

On their return, the buoyant pair soon set up a meeting to create a similar organisation in Birmingham. At the launch meeting held at the Mason's Hotel on Wednesday 8th December 1875, chaired by Carson, the Birmingham and District Football Association was born. It was attended by representatives of eleven clubs, but it was the Calthorpe men who were the real driving force, with strong backing from the Aston Park Unity. Campbell Orr stood for the pivotal role of Secretary, and it was his club that gave the lion's share of the funding to purchase a trophy for the new Association's cup competition. He was keen for the new body to adopt the London F.A. rules, which would have enabled local teams to take part in the English Cup competition (later called the F.A. Cup). Instead a majority voted to adopt the Sheffield rules version, which was more popular locally. Campbell Orr later wrote to Charles Alcock, the F.A. secretary and creator of the F.A. Cup competition, an apologetic note, which was published in the 1876 *Football Annual*. He wrote, "Personally, I much regret that we could not adopt the 'London' rules as they stand....Rather than blame us for introducing new alterations, I think we deserve some credit for attaining unity where the materials were so discordant." Campbell Orr's loyalty was clear.

With an initial membership of just eleven teams, it took a couple of seasons for the new Association to get into its stride. It's cause was not helped by the stance of Birmingham F.C. who seemed to be motivated only by their own self interest. For the 1876/77 season, Webster had already set up further home and away fixtures against the Sheffield F.A. for Quilter's Birmingham F.C. team, and he was not about to let the new local Association takeover his initiative. Although Birmingham F.C. were members of the new Association, it seems that they were just keeping an eye on their perceived rivals from the inside, and were lukewarm in their support. Henry Quilter, their backer, was continuing to use his team as a vehicle for attracting spectators to the Lower Grounds, and was not really interested in the Association for its own sake. Obvious tensions were developing. After the 4-0 defeat in the second game against Sheffield F.A. on 27th December 1875 at Quilter's Lower Grounds, the following letter appeared in the Birmingham Daily Post:

"Sir,
With reference to the match played at Aston Lower Grounds on Monday between Sheffield and Birmingham, will Mr Quilter oblige a few old football players by informing them upon what principle the team that represented Birmingham was chosen; and how many Birmingham clubs were in reality represented?

That Birmingham was disgraced is certain; and not a few think with me that, had a purely representative team been selected from the numerous clubs playing in this town and its immediate vicinity, the result would have been different.

I enclose my card and name of my club, and am, sir
Yours truly
HALF-BACK
New Street, Birmingham, December 28 1875"

This was just three weeks after the formation of the new Birmingham and District Football Association. Pointedly, Campbell Orr, the new secretary, and his Calthorpe team-mate, John Carson, the Association vice-president, no longer featured in the Birmingham F.C. team. It wasn't until the 1877/78 season, by which time a single version of association rules had been agreed between the Sheffield and London associations, that the official Birmingham and District Association managed to organise their own fixture against the Sheffield F.A. *The Sheffield Independent* newspaper reported (25/3/1878), "During the past two seasons, matches have been played by the Sheffield Association with a team selected under the auspices of the Birmingham Club, but as it was this year found that an association had been formed in that town, which was supported by a large number of leading clubs in the district, it was considered by the Sheffield committee that it would be more proper to arrange the fixture with them, and the present match was the first meeting of the two associations."

John Carson was now captain, and the venue was the Aston Unity Ground in Aston Lane, with Quilter's Lower Grounds being snubbed. The 5-0 win for Sheffield remained familiar. However the match was a landmark event for the Birmingham

Association who were now finally recognised in Sheffield as the official voice of football in Birmingham. It had taken over two years to reach this point. During this period the new Association had gradually moved forwards setting up its own cup competition. Being founded partway through the 1875/6 season, there had been insufficient time to arrange a full cup competition during it's first season. Instead a one match exhibition final, with no previous knock out rounds, was organised at Wednesbury Town's (later called Strollers) Crankhall Farm ground between Tipton and Aston Villa, which Tipton won 1-0.

The local Association's second season was more fruitful. Not only did it organise a full cup competition, with sixteen entrants, it also played its first inter Association representative match. The fixture against North Wales District F.A. at Calthorpe's Bristol Road ground on 4th November 1876 ended in a 3-2 defeat, with Charles Crump, the Association President, scoring both goals. Nevertheless, the apparent power struggle between the Association and Birmingham F.C. remained unresolved. Revealingly, Birmingham F.C. was the only club from the eleven who originally founded the Association, not to take part in the inaugural Birmingham Cup competition (1876/77). Back at the Lower Grounds, the club's backer Henry Quilter, was becoming increasingly rattled by the growing clout of the Association, and it's threat to his money making ambitions. What would have really irritated him was the prominence of the Calthorpe duo, James Campbell Orr and John Carson, particularly as their Calthorpe club had hosted the first Birmingham Cup Final at their Bristol Road ground.

Quilter's initial response was to disregard the new Association. For three years his club stubbornly ignored the new cup competition, hoping for it to be a flop. He considered many teams in the Birmingham Cup competition to be third rate and not worth paying to watch. As an experienced sports promoter, he was quite happy to carry on with his approach of booking top teams to turn out at the Lower Grounds to play friendly games against his Birmingham F.C. team. He firmly believed that crowds were attracted purely by the spectacle of watching the best teams. This approach had worked for him initially with cricket fixtures during the late 1860s and early 1870s, and later with football as he plugged into it's growing popularity. What he hadn't realised was the fervour and passion that could be whipped up by competitive matches, no matter what the skill level. He had never had this added dimension within his cricket promotions, and it had caught him by surprise.

The new cup competition gave a new edge to fixtures, generating local rivalry. The prospect of a good cup run and the opportunity to achieve a 'giant killing' started to fire the imagination of the spectators. It was all very well for Quilter to attract top football teams to the Lower Grounds, but the matches were just friendly fixtures, without the intensity of the local cup games. The Birmingham Cup was gaining more entrants with each passing year, and with several attendances of 5,000 or more, the whole issue, no doubt, started to prey on Quilter's mind. By 1878/79 the local competition had attracted twenty-eight teams, including for the first time Small Heath Alliance, and Quilter knew that his policy of remaining aloof from the expanding football community was not working. He had made a mistake and needed to change tack.

For the 1879/80 season, Quilter's Birmingham F.C. finally entered the Birmingham Cup for the first time, and it wasn't just goodwill which had changed his stance. First and foremost he was a businessman. Cleverly he managed to broker a formal agreement with the Birmingham and District F.A. for his Lower Grounds Company to stage various Birmingham Cup matches. The agreement was ratified by the Association members at Nock's Hotel on 3rd December 1879, and between 1880 and 1886, Quilter's Lower Grounds hosted seven consecutive finals, and all but one of the semi-finals, as it became the Association's preferred venue. It's clear that a financial deal had been struck with both parties sharing the profits. With Cup Final crowds frequently near the 10,000 mark and other ties drawing in good crowds, it was a lucrative alignment for both parties. Over the seven year period, the Lower Grounds venue was used on at least thirty-six occasions by the Association. As well as staging finals and semi-finals, the ground hosted many Fourth Round ties and replays, which were routinely held on neutral grounds during this period.

Oddly, Birmingham F.C's 4-1 defeat against Saltley College in 1879, was their sole Birmingham Cup tie. In the following season, 1880/81, the club scratched from the competition, and never entered it again. Not long afterwards, the club's captain and mentor, Henry Haywood Webster emigrated to Australia. As a pre-send off, a special benefit match was arranged for him on 26th August 1882, when his old Wednesday club came down from Sheffield to play Aston Villa at the Lower Grounds. A crowd of 3,000 turned up to watch Sheffield Wednesday win 1-0.

6
EARLY DEVELOPMENTS AT SMALL HEATH ALLIANCE 1876 TO 1878

6.1 THE SUMMER OF 1876

It's the 1876 cricket season which gives us the first hint of the thriving nature of the new Small Heath Alliance club. Only a few days after the conclusion of their first football season, a cricket match between the Alliance Captain's XI and the Alliance Treasurer's XI clearly showed that the burgeoning club already had enough players to support at least two teams. Impressively, throughout the summer, the club was able to field both first and second eleven cricket teams as it's popularity amongst local youths gathered pace. Most of the matches were played on away grounds, such as Aston Park or more frequently Calthorpe Park, a sign that the Alliance club still had problems in accessing a decent playing area within Small Heath.

The opening "Captain's versus Treasurer's" cricket fixture, 8th April 1876, offers vague clues into the club's early organisational set-up. Taken at face value, it denotes that the posts of captain and treasurer were considered the most important. It's not until the following season that an Alliance cricket secretary is first evidenced. An entry in *Sport and Play* (28th March 1877), identifies him as Thomas Hampshire of 6 Norwood Terrace, Bedford Road, Camphill. His title, *cricket* secretary, infers that the club's cricket and football sections each had their own secretary.

The earliest reference I can find of any Alliance football secretary is in the *Midland Athlete* journal dated 28th January 1880, when Billy Edden was in post. The main role of any club secretary, at this time, was to organise fixtures. The captain's position was much more influential, having a key involvement in team selection and tactics.

The following cricket fixtures, for both Small Heath Alliance and the Trinity Choir teams, were found advertised in the *Birmingham Daily Post* throughout the 1876 season, proving that both clubs now existed alongside each other.

SMALL HEATH ALLIANCE CRICKET FIXTURES 1876

Date	Fixture	Venue
8th April	Captain v. Treasurer's Teams of Small Heath Alliance	Small Heath
14th April	1st.XI v. Shakespeare	Calthorpe Park
29th April	1st.XI v. Selly Oak	Selly Oak
	2nd.XI v. Ryland Unity	Calthorpe Park
13th May	1st.XI v. Battery Company	Calthorpe Park
	2nd.XI v. John Wesley	Small Heath
27th May	1st.XI v. Marlborough	Calthorpe Park
17th Jun	1st.XI v. Redditch Windsor Football Players	Calthorpe Park
24th Jun	1st.XI v. Holte	Aston Park
	2nd.XI v. John Wesley	Calthorpe Park
15th Jul	1st.XI v. Battery Company	Calthorpe Park
5th Aug	1st.XI v. Balsall Heath Unity	Calthorpe Park
12th Aug	1st.XI v. Tennyson	Calthorpe Park

TRINITY CHOIR CRICKET FIXTURES 1876

Date	Fixture	Venue
27th May	v. Browne's Green Collegiate School of Hamstead, near Handsworth	Birchfield
7th Aug	v. Summerfield Unity	Summerfield Park
26th Aug	v. Summerfield Park Unity	Summerfield Park

Tantalisingly, we get a glimpse of some Alliance team names from a scorecard for the match against Redditch Windsor Football Players, from the *Worcestershire Chronicle* on 24th June 1876. Billy Edmonds and Tom James were the star bowlers.

<u>Redditch Innings</u>

Bromley	c. W. Johnson	b. T. James	7
E. Merry		b. Edmonds	31
M. Bryant		b. T. James	4
M. Haccox		b. Edmonds	1
Rev. M. Astbury	c. W. Johnson	b. T. James	11
Cox		b. Edmonds	0
J. Fourt	c. R. Johnson	b. T. James	4
F. Merry	not out		6
W. Guise		b. T. James	0
H. Fourt	c. Baugh	b. Edmonds	1

J. H. Avery   run out   1
                              Extras   14
                              TOTAL   80

Small Heath Alliance   TOTAL   58

Redditch won by 22 runs.

Alliance players would also represent the club at local amateur athletic meetings. In June 1878, at the annual Handsworth Athletics sports meeting at Aston Lower Grounds, Tom James represented Small Heath Alliance in the 440 yards running event and was only beaten by a runner from the Birmingham Athletics Club. It seems that the vision of the founders had been to set up an all round sports club.

6.2 ONE SEASON AT LADYPOOL LANE 1876/77

During the summer of 1876, the Alliance club was desperate to seek out a better playing area on which to kick off the new season. The wasteland in Arthur Street had served it's purpose, enabling the club to get up and running, but the use of the land was purely unofficial, and under threat from housing development. After much searching, the club was offered the use of a field a couple of miles away, just off Ladypool Lane in Sparkbrook. It is generally accepted that the club played here for the whole season, although a contemporary newspaper report seems to contradict this long held belief, and needs exploring. The element of doubt is triggered by a report in the *Birmingham Daily Post* concerning the Alliance's last home game of the season against Harborne. It begins, "A match was played on Saturday (17th March) at Small Heath on a field belonging to Mr. Lowe of Whitmore House, who kindly placed it at the service of the Alliance club." This extract, published just three days after the match, seems to suggest that the game was played in Small Heath, not Sparkbrook. The likely explanation is that the report is just badly worded, and could be interpreted as meaning that the game was played at the home of the Small Heath club. This view is corroborated by a pre-match advertisement for the fixture in the *Post* just two days before the game, which gave Ladypool Lane as the venue. It seems highly unlikely that this advertised venue would have changed at such short notice.

This all seems straight forward and fairly conclusive until an end of season summary in the *Sport and Play* weekly journal, listed "Smallheath"(sic) as the venue for the Alliance's final two home games of the season; Walsall Victoria on 10th and Harborne on 17th March. For each of the previous home games, the *Sport and Play* results list gives Ladypool Lane as the venue, so it seems quite a deliberate distinction. This swings the argument back in favour of an earlier return to Small Heath. However, a possible explanation against this, is that the *Sport and Play* journal was merely repeating erroneous details that it picked up from earlier *Daily Post* articles. Either way, there remains an element of doubt. Perhaps more clues can be found by exploring the identity of Mr. Lowe, the owner of the field, and where his field was located.

John Lowe, a sixty-four year old father of twelve, was a well known figure in Small Heath, being a highly successful businessman and ex-Town Councillor. He lived in one of the most prominent residences on the Coventry Road, Whitmore House. Set in a few acres of land, the grand Georgian house had been his home since 1855. Before moving there, he had lived at 8 Highgate, a road adjacent to Ladypool Lane, where he also owned some pastureland for his livestock. He had always shown a keen interest in keeping livestock and poultry, and even helped found the Birmingham and Midland Counties Exhibition of Cattle, Sheep, Pigs and Poultry in 1848. The annual agricultural show grew from strength to strength, drawing in thousands of visitors each year, and even attracted livestock entries from Prince Albert, Queen Victoria's husband. On moving from 8 Highgate, he had retained and continued to use his fields there, but now in his sixties and becoming less energetic, his focus was purely on his Whitmore House estate, where he employed a live in farm servant to look after his livestock and poultry, and a dairymaid. He no longer bothered much with his surplus field in Ladypool Lane, and this is why he was able to let the Alliance club use it. This all tends to suggest that the same field was used for the whole season.

His wealth had been generated by his highly successful manufacturing and wholesale business he ran with his longstanding partner, William Batty Mapplebeck. Aptly named 'Mapplebeck and Lowe', their business made and sold metal furnishings, such as stove grates, kitchen ranges, fenders, and iron and brass bedsteads. The company's premises, in the Bull Ring and Smithfield, boasted the largest stock of heavy ironmongery in the town. Their already flourishing business really took off following their decision to have a stand at the ground breaking 1851 Great Exhibition in London. Their range of goods included weighing machines, drainage pipes and mills. Orders for their goods poured in from all over Britain and overseas, keeping their order books full and bringing in large profits.

Lowe had also been a longstanding political campaigner for the Tories, mainly in an era when they had struggled to gain support in Birmingham, but by the time he lent his field to the Alliance club, his involvement in political activities was on the decline. He had retired from the Town Council in January 1875 and was now less active in public life. Politically, John Lowe had been at his peak during the mid-1860s, when he was elected as the Tory councillor for the St. Peter's Ward. In 1867 he was elected as a Governor of the Children's Hospital alongside Liberal counterpart Joseph Chamberlain, who was later to become Birmingham's celebrated Mayor. It would be wrong, though, to categorise John Lowe as a local Tory big hitter. He was more a dependable party supporter who gained his influence through his business success.

So what might have triggered his generosity to the young men at the Alliance club? It certainly wasn't to pick up any political advantage, as making gestures to gain popularity was no longer on his agenda. His offer to let them use his field seems to have been for purely altruistic reasons. As a longstanding resident of Small Heath, he was happy to give practical help to the team that was proudly representing his neighbourhood. He had a track record of public spiritedness. For example, he donated money to the Birmingham General Dispensary, and used his influence on the organising committee of the annual Birmingham Cattle and Poultry Show to ensure that low price tickets were available to the working classes.

There are also a couple of connections with players from the team, which may have encouraged Lowe's welcome support. Firstly, his business partner, William Mapplebeck, was a Rotherham born grate manufacturer. Could this suggest a possible link with the James family, also born in Rotherham? Mark James, himself a skilled grate and fender fitter, and father of the three James brothers, may have done fitting work for Mapplebeck and Lowe, who sold large numbers of grates and fenders from their Bull Ring emporium. If this idea seems a little tenuous, then John Lowe's connection with the Barmore family may be more convincing. Samuel Barmore, the father of Alliance striker Charlie Barmore, was an active member of the Birmingham Conservative Association, and well known to Lowe. Perhaps it was this link which prompted him to assist the club.

Whatever the truth, the use of John Lowe's field in Ladypool Lane, Sparkbrook, was a piece of unexpected good fortune for the Alliance club, giving them some welcome security as they approached the start of their second season. Ideally the club needed a more permanent base, but for now the new venue gave them a bit of breathing space and enabled them to arrange a full set of fixtures, free from the previous uncertainty of their wasteland pitch in Arthur Street, where, at best, they only had a kind of squatter's rights. The only downside was that it was no longer in Small Heath. The new location, in neighbouring Sparkbrook, was on the other side of the G.W.R. rail track, about a mile and a half south-west of their original pitch.

The first job for the enthusiastic players was to get the field into a fit state for football. Until recently, Mr. Lowe had routinely used the field to graze his cattle. Occasionally he had also used it for pigs, when getting them ready for show. This suggests that the old meadow would have been fairly uneven and undulating, after being churned up by the livestock. No doubt a few weeks before the start of the new season, volunteers from the club would make efforts to get the field into shape, and mark out the pitch ready for it to be roped off from spectators.

The big change for the club was their intention to charge for admission. The entrance fee was set at one old penny, the equivalent of just under half a penny in today's decimal currency, which would be collected at the entrance gate set up on Ladypool Lane. The first Saturday in October was traditionally noted as the opening day of the football season, and in line with this the new ground held it's first game on Saturday 7th October 1876. An advert in the *Birmingham Daily Post* simply said, "Football Fixture at Ladypool Lane, Sparkbrook - Small Heath Alliance v. Wednesbury Old Park", with no start time given. The Old Park club had it's origins in the Black Country town's Old Park Ironworks, and is recorded as playing cricket matches as far back as 1864.

The number of spectators turning up to watch was quite modest. According to the club's 1975 centenary souvenir publication, *One Hundred Years History of Birmingham City Football Club*, the gate money for the first game was just 4 shillings and 3 pence (pre-decimalisation). With each spectator paying one penny entrance, it equates to just fifty-one people. A week earlier, Aston Villa had opened their new Wellington Road enclosure at Perry Barr, also with a game against a Wednesbury club (Wednesbury Town), which attracted a crowd of twenty-one. Ladypool Lane was typical of many early football venues. It was just a "pop up" enclosure in a field with no refinements whatsoever. Watching football in winter from the edge of a muddy field, open to the elements and often wet under foot, was only for the hardy enthusiast. There were no covered areas for spectators or sloping banks to improve viewing, just lumpy grassy areas between the edge of the pitch, cordoned off by a rope, and the field boundary. The only structures were the teams' temporary canvas changing tents, pitched in one corner of the field.

These type of primitive facilities were the norm for all football matches played during the 1870s. Even the F.A. Cup final pitch at Kennington Oval had no viewing stands, being just a roped off area set up within the outfield of Surrey Cricket Club. It took until 1883, after staging ten finals, for the Oval to erect a small stand which gave covered seating to a few hundred spectators. Before this, the only seating was in the horse drawn carriages that some of the more wealthy spectators had paid extra to bring in. The pitch used for the world's first international match, an England versus Scotland fixture at the West of Scotland Cricket ground in Partick in November 1872, was similar, with the two thousand crowd cordoned off from the playing area by a mere perimeter rope. There is evidence that some other sporting events fared better. For the Birmingham Cricket Club Athletic Sports event at Aston Lower Grounds in June 1877, the proprietor Mr. Quilter "had erected a large and comfortable wooden stand for several hundred spectators." (*Birmingham Daily Post* 4th June 1877).

With a first attendance of just fifty-one at Ladypool Lane, it is unlikely that crowd levels grew with any rapidity during the season. Even as spectators got used to the regularity of fixtures, it's likely that crowds remained relatively small, perhaps peaking at between 100 and 150. There was plenty of room for spectators to stand around the pitch without needing to look over anyone's shoulder. In this context, talk of ground capacity is something of a moot point, with no practical significance. Besides, planning regulations and health and safety requirements for such events were virtually non-existent. In theory, the club could have crammed as many people into the field as possible. It's obvious, however, that this was never going to be tested, with only modest numbers ever attending.

At this time, crowds at Villa's Wellington Road home remained sparse. William McGregor, who started watching Villa in 1876, wrote, "Spectators were often few and far between at Wellington Road in the early days. I can recall more than one match where there were only two spectators; myself and George Ramsay's brother." (George Ramsay was the Villa captain).

Small Heath Alliance certainly had a busy fixture list, arranging for most of their early season matches to be held at their new ground. Between October and December 1876, nine of the twelve known fixtures were played at home. The opening game, against Wednesbury Old Park, is said to have marked the Alliance debut of nineteen years old Arthur James, who would later gain recognition as the club's first star player. It also marked the debut for another precocious talent, Old Park's right winger George Holden, just one day after his seventeenth birthday. The two talented wide men were destined to follow impressive careers, both playing several representative games for the Birmingham and District F.A. team. During the 1880s, Holden went on to gain four England caps during a spell with another Wednesbury team, Old Athletic. The unlucky Arthur James' aspirations, on the other hand, would be hindered by more than one serious injury.

Throughout the match, Old Park, in their red shirts, white sleeves and navy shorts, proved to be stubborn opposition. In a tightly fought encounter, the Alliance were defeated by a single goal to nil.

New players were now joining on a regular basis. The average age of the inaugural team had been just over nineteen years, but this soon started to rise as interest in the club spread to an older age group. Prominent among the new influx were two sets of brothers; David and William Purcocks, and George and William Penfield. They were several years older than the other outfield players, and three of them, the Purcocks and George Penfield, were even older than goalkeeper Billy Edden. Besides the added maturity, the new recruits brought a welcome physical presence to the ranks. George and William Penfield were powerfully built, with muscles fine tuned by years of working in a foundry as iron moulders. It was tough uncompromising work, needing both strength and endurance, qualities they could quickly transfer to the football field. With tough men like this, the team was not easily out-muscled or intimidated, giving an added confidence to the younger players. The Burton born Penfields remained dependable stalwarts throughout the 1870s, and on at least one occasion William stepped in as captain when Arthur James was away on representative duty for the Birmingham F.A. Team (late in the 1878/79 season). Both Penfield's retired from playing at the end of the 1879/80 season, with George remaining involved with the team on the coaching side. He was still trainer of the first team when the club reached the F.A. Cup semi-final in 1886.

The Birmingham football scene was now developing at a rapid rate. The creation of the town's first knock out cup competition, ready for the start of the 1876/77 season, just added to the excitement, and the inaugural competition attracted sixteen local clubs. Organised by the recently formed Birmingham and District F.A., all the cup ties were to be played on a twelve a side basis, using Sheffield rules. This was at odds with the official Football Association in London, whose English Cup Competition (the F.A. Cup), stipulated eleven a side. None of the local clubs gave this a second thought, as no team in the town had ever entered the English Cup, a situation which would remain unchanged for the next three years. Something had to give in the future, but for now Sheffield rules had been cemented as the dominant force within the Birmingham area by the local Association. This local standardisation was an important step forward, as, for the first time, it encouraged teams to adopt one format across the district.

For the Alliance club though, the new Birmingham Cup competition had come too soon. Still in their infancy, the competition had coincided with the upheaval of their move to Ladypool Lane, and they knew they weren't ready for it. Their 1876/77 fixture list included games against five clubs who had entered the new local cup competition; Wednesbury Old Park, their season's opening opponents, Aston Park Unity, Harborne, Harold and Walsall Victoria Swifts. This in itself adds strength to the assertion that the Alliance club was favouring the Sheffield rules version of the game.

The furthest they ventured during the season was to play a return fixture at Redditch Windsor on 24th February 1877. The Alliance's ties with the Worcestershire team seem to have been well developed. During the previous summer, 1876, they had visited Redditch to play cricket. Then in November of the same year, the Redditch Windsor football team had been one of the earliest visitors to Ladypool Lane. In this fixture, according to the *Worcestershire Chronicle*, the Redditch team had played with thirteen players. The Redditch Windsor team was: W. Guise (capt.), T. Evans, T. Guise, H. Eames, J. C. Cross, J. Adams (forwards); F. Ford, R. Aston, F. Dobbins, T. Gibbons, A. Hill, E. Merry (backs); T. Hemmings (goal).

There were no details of the Alliance team, so we can only speculate on whether it was a thirteen a side game, or if the Alliance men simply allowed the Redditch team the benefit of an extra man. It seems that the Alliance men were happy to be flexible, and were not overly concerned about the local Association's preference for twelve a side. In any case, it would be another two years before they joined it. At first glance, these cordial links with Redditch Windsor seem mildly curious. The probable explanation lies in a family connection to the area linked to the three Edden brothers. Their step-mother, Maria Edden (nee Hawthorn) was born in Redditch, and her marriage to their father, Thomas, had taken place in Redditch in 1857. It is likely that the whole family were regular visitors to Redditch, with the matches growing out of these ties. This would certainly help to explain the Alliance's apparent relaxed approach to the team numbers.

Team line ups for any matches prior to 1879 are rare to find. The earliest I came across was in the *Sport and Play* journal dated 14th March 1877, for a 12 aside encounter against Walsall Victoria Swifts. The line up was:

T. James(captain), W. Edden, G. Edden, A. James, F. James, W. Penfield, G. Penfield, Purcocks, Rowe, Carter, Sparrow and Hardes.

It's interesting to note that Thomas James was captain, with no involvement of Billy Edmonds. The game ended goal less, with the *Birmingham Post* reporting that, "Messrs. A. James, W. Penfield, T. Hardes and G. Penfield played in capital style for the Alliance, with some clever play by W. Purcock (sic)"

A week later, the team against Harborne, as listed in the *Birmingham Post*, was:
T. James, A. James, F. James, T. Hardes, W. Penfield, G. Penfield, T. Hampshire, J. Sparrow, W. Edden, G. Edden, W. Purcock (sic), and D. Purcock (sic).

The fact that Thomas James was the first listed indicates that he was again captain. In a 4-0 win, Arthur James scored a hat trick and Hardes the other.

Nationally, the argument between the two dominant Associations, Sheffield and London, on which code to adopt was about to come to a head. It was the high profile games between representative teams from different local Associations that began to put most pressure on the need to agree a single set of association rules. A series of matches played between representative teams from Sheffield and London highlighted the problem perfectly. From 1871/72 to 1876/77, the Sheffield and London teams played several home and away fixtures, using the home team's rules. Needless to say Sheffield won all six of their home games using Sheffield rules, and London remained unbeaten in their home games under London F.A. rules, winning four and drawing two. This sequence of predictable results was perfect ammunition for those seeking a single set of rules for all association football matches. Stuart G. Smith, captain of the Manchester F.A. contributed the following letter to *The Field Magazine* in March 1877, which neatly summed up the frustrations felt by most football followers.

"......I think that I may safely say that there is not any district in which the inconvenience of having two different codes of Association rules is felt more than here, where if a club adopt one, no matter which, it is obliged to get matches with clubs playing the other, and has to play different rules, when away, from those which it plays on its own ground. Look at the results of the two London and Sheffield matches this season, each side having it their own way at their own rules. Had there been only one code of rules, and both sides accustomed to them, what would have been the results? No one, I think, will deny that it is more enjoyable to play a closely contested game than to gain an easy victory or to suffer a hollow defeat......."

In the previous month the Sheffield F.A. had agreed to the London F.A's three man offside rule, which had been used by the F.A. since 1866. Up until this agreement, the Sheffield rules had used a more liberal offside rule. As long as the attacker received the ball with the goalkeeper between him and the goal line, in Sheffield rules he was not offside. It was on the issue of throw-ins where agreement couldn't be reached. Sheffield rules retained kick-ins from the touchline, instead of throw-ins, but by the end of April 1877 the Sheffield F.A. decided to accept the following proposal which had earlier been submitted by the Clydesdale club from Scotland:

"When the ball is in touch a player from the opposite side to that which kicked it out shall throw it from the point in the boundary line where it left the ground in any direction the thrower may choose. The ball must be thrown at least six yards and shall be in play when thrown in, but the player throwing it shall not play it until it has been played by another."

At last, with an agreement made on throw-ins, there was just one code of association football in England, ready for the start of the 1877/78 season. Teams and local Associations would no longer need to choose between the two versions. Crucially, this meant that the Birmingham Cup competition would now be in sync with the F.A. Cup; both on an eleven a side footing.

Even though the Alliance club was only drawing in a sprinkling of spectators to Ladypool Lane, the residents in the nearby houses couldn't fail to notice their presence. On match days the sounds of players shouting to each other during the game, and the constant thud of the heavy leather ball as they crunched into tackles would reverberate around the local streets. One nearby resident was Sam Gessey, who would later become a pivotal figure in the club's move back to Small Heath. He lived in Main Street just a couple of streets from the Ladypool Lane pitch, with his wife and young family.

A keen sportsman, he had regularly been turning out for the nearby St. Luke's football club, who, like many early teams, played their fixtures at Calthorpe Park. Even though he was now thirty-one, an age by which many footballers had decided to hang up their boots, Sam Gessey had kept himself in good shape and was still giving solid performances at full back. As a fellow footballer, he had naturally been keeping a keen eye on the rival Alliance team, and after discovering their eagerness to move back to their Small Heath heartland, he knew that he was in a position to help. As chance would have it, he had recently acquired the use of some fields there, on a long term lease, and was willing to rent one of them to the Alliance club. The land was in an ideal location right in the centre of Small Heath, just off the main Coventry Road thoroughfare, at the junction with Muntz Street. An agreement was reached by the club to pay him a yearly rental of £5, enabling them to move in time for the start of the 1877/78 season. It was Arthur James who reputedly signed the paperwork on the deal, perhaps indicating that he was the de facto secretary of the club during this period. The conjecture is that he followed on from Billy Edmonds.

6.3 THE RETURN TO SMALL HEATH AT GESSEY'S FIELD 1877

Initially just an open field, the new Muntz Street ground would be the club's home for the next twenty-nine years. Although it had taken a big step forward in returning home to Small Heath, it was back to square one in terms of the hard work needed to get the field ready for football. The disruption caused by the third change of grounds in as many years meant that the club's focus was purely on getting set for the new season. An important task was to ensure that the team had a full fixture list. The number of new teams coming onto the scene was growing with each passing month, giving the club plenty of options. As well as matches against some old friends like Walsall Victoria, Redditch Windsor, Nechells, and Harborne, several fixtures were set up against the newer clubs. Amongst them were the Arcadians club, Heathfield (Handsworth), and the Lion Works. There was no time to think about joining the local Association, or entering any cup competitions. It was all hands to the pump, fencing off the ground and dealing with the rough playing surface. Recalling his trips to the new enclosure in 1877, a *Sports Argus* football writer called "Nomad" wrote in 1916, "In those days I had merely to climb over a fence opposite the house in which I lived, cut over a couple of fields, and I was on the Alliance ground." Just this one sentence gives a strong sense of the semi-rural feel of the area. Two edges of the Alliance enclosure were flanked by open meadowland; the touchline furthest from the Coventry Road, and the goal line furthest from Muntz Street. Soon after the Alliance's arrival, a local junior team, St. Andrew's Sunday School, started using the field next door. They remained neighbours until early 1884, when Charles Road was cut through from Coventry Road right across the middle of the Sunday School pitch, forcing them to leave.

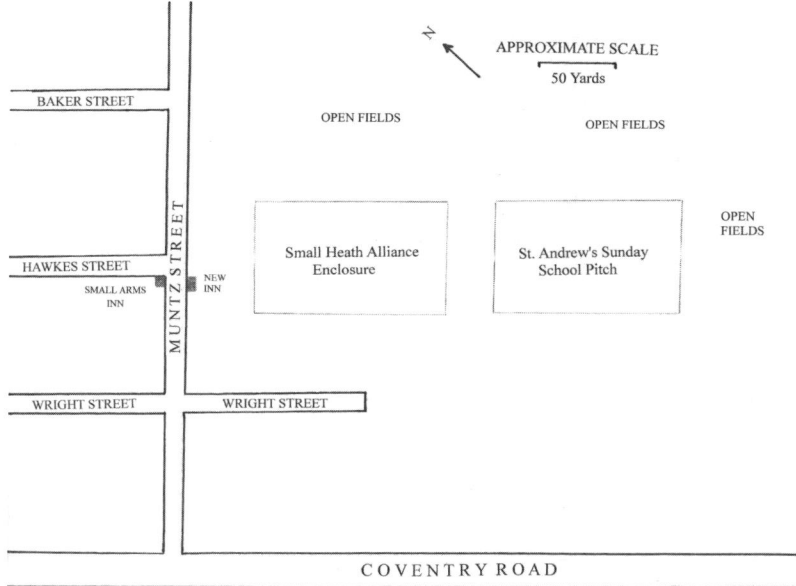

The Muntz Street Enclosure as it was until 1883.

It was in his native Oxford that the new Alliance landlord, Sam Gessey, first developed his love of sport. He was born and raised in Summer Town, a village on the Banbury Road on the northern edge of Oxford, where his father was a farm labourer. In 1863, as an eighteen year old, Sam played cricket for the newly established Summer Town club, by which time he was into the fourth year of his carpentry apprenticeship. A keen cricketer, he was a regular in the Summer Town team for nearly a decade, playing at venues such as the Brasenose ground on the Abingdon Road, and at Witney and Islip. In between cricket, he took part in local athletic sports events. In April 1868, for example, he competed in the hurdle race at the athletics event in Witney. There is no evidence that he played football in Oxford, but an interesting possibility is that he was inspired by the notorious Oxford University football team of the early 1870s, which played it's matches at the nearby University Parks ground on the Banbury Road, not far from the Gessey family home in Summer Town. Founded in 1872, the Oxford University Association Football Club was one of the dominant forces in the early years of the F.A. Cup. It's likely that Sam got to see the famous team, along with his four younger brothers, as it embarked on its first impressive cup run. The top teams of the day, such as Crystal Palace (not linked to the current club) and the Royal Engineers, were defeated at the Parks ground, as the University team made it through to the 1873 final.

Not long afterwards, around 1874, Sam moved to Sparkbrook in Birmingham with his wife and young daughter. Later that year, the Oxford University team again got through to the final, this time winning the F.A Cup as they beat the Royal Engineers 2-0 at the Kennington Oval. No doubt Sam would read about the triumph of his old local team, as he settled into his new Sparkbrook surroundings. He now worked at a Tin Plates Works in Charles Henry Street. The factory employed around forty "men and boys", and it seems that Sam was soon given the responsibility of taking on new workers. A 'situations vacant' from the *Birmingham Daily Post* in June 1874 read, "Wanted a youth about 17 to assist in a manufactory. Must be well behaved and respectable. Apply S. Gessey. Messrs. H.J. Hookham and Sons, Charles Henry Street." At this time, Sam was still making the occasional sortie back to his rural haunts to play village cricket. In September 1875, he played for Appleton, a village on the Oxfordshire-Berkshire borders, against Fyfield. Appleton was the home village of his wife Mary Ann, and he played in the team with two of her brothers, George and Arthur Holifield.

The first match at the new Muntz Street enclosure was against Saltley College on 11th September 1877. In front of sparse crowd of barely fifty onlookers, the visitors were easily brushed aside 5-0. The gate receipts were 6 shillings and 8 pence. In a barnstorming season, the Alliance were a formidable force at Muntz Street, beating Lion Works 9-0, Walsall Swifts 10-0 and St. Luke's 10-0. They also recorded an 8-0 victory at Coventry. Throughout the season, the Alliance team proved unbeatable, home and away, notching up 108 goals and conceding only 11 in a twenty-two game schedule.

7

PROGRESS GATHERS PACE 1878 TO 1881

7.1 THE FIRST COMPETITIVE FIXTURE 1878/79

After three years existence, which had seen the club change grounds each season, it was a welcome advantage to be able to remain at the same place for consecutive seasons. Organisationally the club now had the scope to plan ahead with more ambition, and finally felt the time was right to join the local Football Association. For once the players had a sense of security, no longer dogged by the uncertainties caused by the lack of a permanent base. The Muntz Street ground gave them an extra spring in their step, generated by their previous season's unbeaten run there. Like so often in football, however, things didn't go as planned, and the pre-season optimism was soon dampened by some early disappointments.

One of these was an unexpected home defeat to the Walsall team, Trinity Club of Caldmore, who incidentally featured a seventeen year old Alf Jones, making his first team debut. He would later develop into a fine defender, playing a handful of games for England and captaining Walsall Swifts. The young Trinity Club team pulled off a big surprise by winning 2-1 to put a dent into the Alliance's proud home record and spoil their air of invincibility. Recalling details some thirty-five years after the event, Alf Jones commented that the Alliance "were a much older team, many with long whiskers. What we lacked in size, we made up for with cleverness." (*Walsall Advertiser*, 7th February 1914)

Another setback came in the club's first ever competitive fixture. Their membership of the Birmingham and District F.A. had given them entry to the prestigious Birmingham Cup. The 1878/79 competition, now in it's third year, had attracted twenty-eight teams, and the first round draw gave the Alliance a tough home tie against Calthorpe, one of the most influential clubs in the town. Played on 9th November 1878, the takings for the game were a splendid £2/18/2d (source: *Association Football and the Men who made it* - Gibson and Pickford, 1906). If the admission price was 2d each, this would give an attendance of 349.

Despite losing 1-0 and the blow of falling at the first hurdle, it wasn't all doom and gloom. For goalkeeper Billy Edden, there was a positive spin-off. His impressive performance had been admired by two senior figures from the Calthorpe club, John Carson and John Campbell-Orr, both on the committee of the Birmingham and

District F.A. As a newly paid up members, players from the Alliance club were now eligible to be selected for the high profile inter Association representative games, and Billy Edden's eye catching display earned him an immediate call-up to the team.

Just three weeks later, at the Kennington Oval, he made his representative debut against a handy London F.A. team. The captain of the Birmingham F.A. team that day was A.E. Daniell, another Calthorpe man who had witnessed Edden's prowess at close quarters during the earlier cup tie. The representative match, however, proved a tough baptism for the Alliance stopper, with his team crashing 8-0. Despite the one-sided score line, Edden acquitted himself well. *The Birmingham Post* praised his performance saying that "the goalkeeper (Edden) especially proved himself both plucky and clever".

During these early games the wooden cross-bar was not yet in use, even for the high profile representative matches. For now a simple tape was tied to each goal post, eight feet above the ground, an arrangement which survived until the start of the 1882/83 season when wooden cross-bars became compulsory. Goal nets weren't introduced until a few years later in 1891/92.

The Birmingham F.A. team for Edden's debut match was:
W. Edden (Small Heath Alliance) goalkeeper; D. Rutherford (Saltley College) and T. Butler (Aston Unity) backs; A.E. Daniell (Calthorpe, captain) and Sam Page (Wednesbury Old Athletic) half-backs; H. Goodyear (Saltley College) and A. Brown (Aston Unity) left forwards; A.T. Ward (Shrewsbury) and Roland Morley (Wednesbury Old Athletic) centres; W. Bushell (Calthorpe) and George H. Holden (Wednesbury Old Athletic) right forwards.

Alliance player, Arthur James, was also on the radar of the Association selectors, being noted for his speed and trickery. The team performance against the London F.A. had been criticised in the local press for "a lack of dash and pace", and James was quickly drafted into the team just two weeks later for the game at Bramall Lane against an experienced Sheffield F.A. team. Unfortunately the Birmingham F.A. team was on the end of another football lesson, soundly beaten 10-0 by a vastly superior team.

Again, it was a tough game for goalkeeper Billy Edden, the last line of defence in a team that was completely outplayed. The Sheffield press, though, praised him for his brave play. *The Sheffield Independent* reported that "Edden saved his charge by some really plucky play, after being heavily charged by Woodcock". The rules offered little protection to goalkeepers, allowing them to be charged and impeded even when the ball was not close by. They needed to be strong both physically and mentally to survive.

Also in the Birmingham F.A. team that day, making his debut, was defender Sam

Gessey, who as the landlord of the Muntz Street pitch was well known to Billy Edden and Arthur James. However, after the heavy defeat the veteran St. Luke's player, then aged thirty-three, was never picked for representative duty again. Early in the New Year, the Alliance arranged a match with Sam Gessey's St. Luke's club, and in a tight match at Calthorpe Park, the Alliance came out on top 2-1.

For the next inter Association game, against the Scotch Counties on 18th January 1879, Billy Edden lost his place to the Stafford Road Works goalkeeper, E. Ray, with Arthur James the sole remaining Alliance representative. The match at Hampden Park, home of the pioneering Queens Park club, ended in another drubbing for the Birmingham F.A. team as they lost 7-1 on a pitch covered in several inches of snow. The result was further proof that the standard of play in the Birmingham district was lagging behind that of the best Association teams. The fixture against the Scotch Counties had, no doubt, been set up by John Carson, the ex-Queens Park player. Two years earlier, he had already taken the Calthorpe club up to Hampden Park to play against his old club.

Back at the Alliance, their match at Walsall Victoria Swifts on 15th February 1879 ended in disarray, caused by a disagreement over an equalising "goal" claimed by the Swifts. With five minutes to go and Alliance one goal ahead, Billy Edden caught a Swifts' shot a couple of feet from his goal line, and immediately threw the ball down field. At this point, the Swifts' umpire claimed that Edden had allowed the ball to cross his goal line. The Alliance umpire, T. Page, argued that the Swifts' official could not have possibly seen the goal line from where he was standing, and a heated dispute ensued. Dramatically, with neither side willing to give way, the Alliance players put on their coats and left the field, in what was to become a major diplomatic incident.

Adding fuel to the fire, accusations flew from the Walsall crowd that the Small Heath men had improperly borrowed Tom Whitehead from the Stafford Road Works club to strengthen their team. This cut little ice with most football observers as it was well known that Whitehead was a member of both clubs, and that in any case, it was a generally accepted practise that an amateur player was free to play for more than one club. In the heat of the moment, the usual good relations between the two clubs were soured, and in the words of Billy Edden the issue "prevented their Secretaries from making their usual fixtures" for the following 1879/80 season.

Teams from Walsall were now providing the Alliance with plenty of fixtures, with five of the season's last six opponents coming from the town; Victoria Swifts, St. Matthew's Institute, Walsall Athletic (twice), and Walsall Florence. Only Walsall Florence managed to avoid defeat, and that on a day when the Alliance were weakened by the absence of their captain, Arthur James, who was playing for the "English" in an unusual representative game, the "English" versus the "Scotch" at

Aston Lower Grounds. The match had been organised by the local F.A., with both teams selected from players from within the district. The "Scotch" team, which triumphed 4-3, included John Campbell Orr and John Carson, and their umpire was William McGregor, who would later find fame as the founder of the Football League. With no Arthur James in the Alliance team, it was William Penfield, the younger of the two Penfield brothers, who stepped in as captain for their trip to Folly House Lane against Florence.

The 1878/79 season also marked the arrival of two teenage brothers, John Starcke Harlow and Peter William Harlow, who were destined to play a big part in the development of the club. J.S.Harlow soon broke into the first team as a forward, becoming a regular selection over the next three seasons, although never fully cementing his place. His younger brother P.W. Harlow, was mainly confined to second team duties, but it was off the field where he was set to make his biggest impact, serving as one of the club's most innovative and ambitious secretaries. He was responsible for entering the club into the F.A. Cup for the first time in 1881.

The Harlow brothers were the third generation of their family to work in the printing trade, both working as compositors. They were following in the footsteps of their grandfather, John Harlow, who ran a printing business from a shop in Summer Lane during the 1830s and 1840s, and their father, John Tertius Harlow, a newspaper printer. Their father was also heavily involved in the Trades Union movement, and his high profile work as secretary of the Birmingham Trades Council helped to inspire his sons to think progressively at the Alliance club.

At the end of the season, the Alliance members took part in their annual handicap steeplechase, a sort of sporting cum social event starting at the New Inn in Muntz Street and ending at the Plume of Feathers in Miles Street. Although the two pubs were only about a mile apart, the club members were sent on a testing eight mile circuitous route between the two, organised by two so-called "hares", Vincent Teychenne and Arthur Wright. Arthur Wright, a founding player from the club's first teamsheet, was still actively involved with the club, although his playing days were few and far between. His last known appearance had been in goal for the second team versus Asbury at Muntz Street earlier in the season. Young Vincent Teychenne, the brother-in-law of founder David Keys, was approaching his seventeenth birthday. It would be another two seasons before he made his first team debut.

The New Inn in Muntz Street c.1975

The finish of the steeplechase, the Plume of Feathers in Miles Street, was the club's early H.Q. It was right in the heart of where many players lived. William Penfield actually lived in Miles Street, which was adjoined by Bordesley Park Road, where Joe Sparrow, George Edden, captain Arthur James and his brother Fred all resided. No doubt the exhausting event ended with a few beers at their favourite hostelry. It's interesting that the steeplechase was billed as an annual event, suggesting that it had taken place in previous years.

The event shows that cross country running was another sport which was catching on in the district, and it was around this time that a local athletics club, Small Heath Harriers, first appeared on the scene. Cross country running was their main focus, and the landscape around Small Heath was well suited to this, with plenty of farm land and open meadows still remaining. The first recorded race organised by the new Harriers club took place on 11th October 1879, a fortnight into the new football season, starting at the Sydenham Hotel in Golden Hillock Road. Thirteen members ran an eight mile cross country course, ending at the Three Horse Shoes pub in Sheldon.

The Sydenham Hotel was also used by the local rugby club, Small Heath F.C., who used the grounds at the rear, although how long this arrangement lasted is not certain. Then in the early 1880s, it was used as a base by the Centaur Bicycle Club. Previously, throughout the late 1860s and early 1870s, the hotel had been best known for it's pleasure gardens, charging a 2d. admission. Perhaps the proprietor, James Capewell, once harboured visions of matching the facilities at Quilter's Lower Grounds in Aston.

The Plume of Feathers in Miles Street c.1975. This was the early H.Q. of the club, with committee meetings held in a back room.

7.2 THE ALLIANCE CAUSE A SEISMIC CUP SHOCK 1879/80

For the new season, a face familiar to many Alliance players joined the playing staff. It was Sam Gessey, the landlord of the club's ground, who made the switch from his usual St. Luke's team. By this time he was already thirty-four years old, an age by which most footballers had long given up playing, but remarkably for this era, he remained a regular in the team for the next five years. He was several years older than any other team mate. The nearest to him was the evergreen George Penfield at four years younger. Even the most senior founder, Billy Edden, was five years Gessey's junior. This helps to explain why, in some accounts, Gessey is given the nickname "Father Sam".

In the previous season, he had seen his former club scratch from the first round of the Birmingham Cup, whilst witnessing the rise of the Alliance club; better organised and more ambitious than his old club. His role as landlord since 1877, had also helped to foster his growing affinity for the Small Heath set up. His move wasn't to do with money. Football was still a fiercely amateur sport, fitted in around work, with players carrying on their usual jobs throughout the week and usually on Saturday mornings. The players were just ordinary members of the community, trying their best to support their families.

Behind the scenes, goalkeeper Billy Edden was voted to the post of honorary secretary by the club members. As one of the best known players in the district, and an occasional member of the Birmingham Association team, his football contacts would be invaluable in helping to secure prestigious fixtures.

On the pitch, it was a breakthrough season for the Alliance, the one which really brought the club to the notice of the local footballing elite. The club's instant notoriety was created on 25th October 1879 with a stunning 2-1 victory in the Birmingham Cup against the holders and two times winners, Wednesbury Old Athletic. The result was the biggest cup upset ever seen in the district, regarded as the competition's first ever giant killing.

Just a few weeks before the upset, the Alliance had already come across the formidable Old Athletic team in a pre-season football tournament organised by the Aston Villa Cricket and Football Club at their Wellington Road ground in Perry Barr. The ten team contest, played on a six aside basis, included several top teams from the area, such as Calthorpe, Walsall Swifts and Nottingham Forest. The Alliance six aside team was: A. James, Clayton, Hards, Gessey, T. James and W. Edden. After a packed schedule of games, watched by three hundred sodden spectators in a continuous downpour, the Nottingham Forest team took home the 10 guineas first prize by beating Old Athletic in the final. For the Alliance team, routinely beaten by the Old Athletics in the opening round of matches, there was no hint of the amazing drama that was to follow when the teams next met in the Birmingham Cup, a month later.

Interestingly, the six aside tournament seems to have been the first sporting contact between the Alliance club and their future rivals, Aston Villa. Although the two didn't face each other during the contest, there's little doubt that the players would have become acquainted during the afternoon's proceedings as they sheltered from the incessant rain, and it wasn't long before they had set up a fixture. It was a benefit match for Alliance player Fred James, who had broken his arm. The match took place just two weeks later, on 27th September 1879, when the Villa team visited Muntz Street for the historic first encounter. At this time, the two clubs didn't consider themselves to be great rivals, with the greater intensity only surfacing in 1886, following the Alliance's epic cup run through to the F.A. Cup semi-final.

So with the rivalry yet to be developed, it is doubtful whether the crowd totalled more than a few hundred spectators for the game, which resulted in a victory for the Alliance by "one goal and a disputed goal to nil". Disputed goals were a feature of many games during this period. Crucially a goal needed to be supported by both umpires; one being supplied by the home team, and the other by the visitors. So although the Alliance had claimed two goals, one of them had failed to get the agreement of both umpires. In these circumstances the Alliance captain, Arthur

James, would have followed the accepted protocol by allowing the game to be restarted "under protest". This enabled the game to get moving again, whilst accepting that the score would only be classed as a "disputed goal". In most cases the umpires would come to an agreement before the dispute had reached this stage, although some disagreements were inevitable. Arguments over whether the ball had actually passed between the goal posts, or under the tape could be the most contentious. Without goal nets it was often hard to be completely sure if the ball had passed through the goal.

The Alliance team for this historic fixture was: Jack Bodenham (goalkeeper), Gessey, most likely Sam, Tom James, George Penfield, George Edden, Arthur James, Walter Hards, H. Jackson, T. Page, Edwin Booth, and Harry Clayton. *The Midland Athlete* dated 1st October 1879 lists Gessey as G. Gessey, but I suspect that this is a mistake. Errors on the team line ups were not uncommon, as they were transcribed from written team sheets provided by each club after the game, often in poor handwriting. The names could easily be misread by the typesetter, misspelt or wrongly input. Sam Gessey was the regular back for the whole of the season, after his switch from St. Luke's, and this would have been his first appearance for the Alliance. George, his younger brother didn't become involved until the 1880/81 season. The Villa club only turned up with ten men, and it was only some inspired rearguard defending which prevented the score from being much higher. Alliance goalkeeper Jack Bodenham had only just joined the club, immediately standing in for the absent Will Edden. The twenty-one year old Bodenham, a carpenter who lived in Cherrywood Lane, became the regular second team goalkeeper, making about half a dozen first team appearances during the season, as Edden's understudy.

Afterwards both sets of players vented their concerns about the state of the Muntz Street pitch, which was said to be in a furrowed and terribly uneven state. William McGregor, the Villa vice-president, later wrote, "It's furrows were as pronounced as any you would see in the district."(*The Book of Football*, 1906). The heavy rainfall during the previous few weeks had simply added to the atrocious condition of the pitch, as the heavy mud churned up. The Alliance officials were committed to improving the playing surface, but the core problem was caused by the underlying geology of heavy clay, which was never going to be easily sorted. In wet conditions the pitch would inevitably resemble a quagmire, with heavy mud sticking to the players' boots. Conversely, after dry sunny periods the clay would set rock hard, making it just as hazardous. It was a situation which was to plague the club throughout it's time at Muntz Street. Any attempt to alleviate the problem, would be hampered, time and time again, by the naturally occurring clay. Not that Muntz Street was the only ground with problems. Terrible pitches were a routine feature of many early fixtures. Recalling these early times, a prominent local player, Alf Jones of Walsall Swifts, observed, "In my day every club played upon ground which had been a ridge and furrow field, and it was most difficult to keep command of the ball."

Fred James' broken arm kept him out of action for the opening two months of the new season, and while he was on the mend, he spent several matchdays umpiring for the second team, before rejoining first team action on 22nd November against Walsall Athletic.

A week after the Villa encounter, the Alliance team made the short trip to Sam Gessey's old club St. Luke's, who now used a pitch in Brighton Road. It must have been mixed emotions for Sam as his new club trounced his old team mates 16-0, with four Alliance players getting hat tricks; Arthur James 4 goals, Harry Clayton 4, Walter Hards 3, and John Harlow 3. As if the 16-0 humiliation wasn't enough, immediately after the game the Alliance club also poached one of their opponent's brightest prospects, a young Bill Slater. He had put in such an impressive performance, even during the one-sided mismatch, that the following week he walked straight into the Alliance first team. His acquisition was a huge slice of luck for the club. Later in his career he would guide the Alliance to their first ever trophy, the Walsall Cup, when he stood in as captain for the injured Arthur James during the 1882/83 season.

The big match against Wednesbury Old Athletic in the first round of the Birmingham Cup, was originally drawn to take place on the notorious Muntz Street pitch. It was an exciting prospect for the Alliance club to be hosting the best team in the district in only their second competitive game. Most observers were predicting an easy win for the visiting cup holders, when the curious news came through that they had offered the Alliance club a £5 payment to shift the tie to the Wednesbury Oval. So was it just a case of avoiding the Muntz Street pitch? After all, the last time Wednesbury Old Athletic had played a first round tie away from home, they had hammered Harborne 13-0. Surely they weren't fearful of a trip to Small Heath.

It later transpired that the real reason for the switch was to make it easier for the Old Athletic players to attend the wedding of team mate John "Jack" Reeves to his bride Susan Janes, which was taking place on the morning of the match. The last thing his team wanted was the nuisance of a trek over to Small Heath almost immediately afterwards. St. Mark's Church Ocker Hill, where the ceremony was taking place, was just a couple of miles down the road from the rearranged venue of Wednesbury Oval. The Old Athletic team could now enjoy the celebrations before making their way to the ground at the last possible moment. There, an expectant crowd of nearly two thousand Wednesbury folk waited for their heroes to begin the defence of their trophy. In their minds the result was a foregone conclusion. In thirteen previous Birmingham Cup matches, stretching over a three year period, the Old Athletics had only ever lost on one occasion. The Alliance team, on the other hand, were complete cup novices, playing in what was only their second competitive game.

Bravely, the intrepid Alliance men produced one of the greatest cup shocks of the era by pulling off a surprising 2-1 victory. Walter Hards put the Alliance ahead after twenty-five minutes, only for Old Athletic to equalise before half-time, through Morley. In the second half, as so often, it was Arthur James who ran through to score the winning goal for the Alliance. In a tense finish, Billy Edden performed heroics in goal as he beat out shot after shot during a desperate last few minutes. The result left the Wednesbury crowd stunned, and sent ripples of disbelief across the district's football community. That wasn't the end of the intriguing story, though, as some years later George Holden, a member of the beaten team, revealed what really caused the upset. In his reminiscences, he explained that following the wedding celebrations, only two of his team mates had remained sober for the cup tie, allowing the Alliance team to shatter their air of invincibility. The match had also kindled a fierce sense of rivalry between the clubs, with the Old Athletics out to get revenge for their humiliation. In a two year period, between December 1881 and November 1883, the clubs were to face each other on six occasions in a variety of cup matches as the rivalry intensified.

In the next round, the Alliance were drawn to play at home against Aston Unity. The tie, held on 13th December 1879, attracted a bumper crowd of 900, at the time the biggest attendance ever seen at Muntz Street, swelled by the team's heroics in the previous round. On top of that, the Alliance team had won their opening nine games of the season, scoring forty-eight goals and conceding only five. Even though Aston Unity were considered the more senior club with a strong reputation, the Alliance men were confident of claiming another cup scalp. The experienced Aston Unity players seemed sufficiently concerned about the match to indulge in an early example of gamesmanship. Just before kick off, they lodged an objection into the type of footwear used by the Alliance team. Normally, they wore what were termed "slips", which were attached to their shoes to help them keep a better grip. The last minute objection left them with no time to get alternative boots, and without the "slips", they were put at a great disadvantage in the slippery conditions.

Pluckily, they kept the game scoreless until partway through the second half, when Unity claimed a goal which was disputed by the Alliance umpire, Tom Edden. Inexplicably, the referee, Mr. Porter of Calthorpe F.C., failed to decide on the pitch if the goal should stand, and bizarrely referred the incident to the committee of the Birmingham and District F.A. Imagine the chaos today if such a procedure was adopted. In 1879 clarity for spectators was not even a consideration. Five minutes before the end, the Alliance scored a well worked goal when Arthur James squared the ball for Hards to finish.

Amazingly, neither the Alliance players or the home crowd knew whether their team had progressed to the next round. Presumably most of the home crowd thought that their team had triumphed. The score stood at one goal to the Alliance and a "disputed" goal to Unity, which would normally signify a win for the Alliance. Due to the referee's incompetence, however, the teams were forced to wait for several days for a decision. Eventually the Association decided that the match should be replayed, robbing the Alliance of victory. Whether the Unity players had put any pressure on the referee to defer his decision we don't know, but it's certainly the case that as the more senior team and a founding member of the Association, they would naturally have more clout with the Association committee.

The whole episode is a good illustration of how the extra competitiveness of the knock out cup games was gradually eroding the standards of sportsmanship. The sporting ethos of "fair play" and playing "for the love of the game" was now under threat. It was just human nature. The apparent antics of the Unity team to gain an advantage, in first complaining about the Alliance's footwear and then failing to accept the call on the pitch of a "disputed" goal, shows how sporting behaviour can be undermined when the stakes are raised in competitive fixtures.

The replay at Aston Lane, ordered by the local Association, didn't go well for the Alliance. The omens weren't good from the start, with most of the team arriving late. It was hardly ideal preparation as they rushed to the dressing tent to quickly get ready. Most amateur players still worked on Saturday mornings and getting away on time wasn't always possible if a job overran. Players frequently needed to dash straight from work to the game. In the previous month, several Alliance players had arrived late at Muntz Street for the fixture with Excelsior, leading to a forty-five minute delay in the kick-off and causing the game to finish in near darkness. It was just an accepted hazard of early amateur football. With no way of informing team mates about delays, everyone, including the crowd, was resigned to hanging around until any absent players finally arrived.

When the replay against Unity eventually kicked off at 3.15p.m., the Alliance were still a man short and forced to play the first fifteen minutes with only ten men. Inevitably the extra effort required by the ten men started to tell, and in a first half spell Unity went three goals up. Doggedly the Small Heath men clawed back two goals, before Unity once again went three goals clear. As the daylight faded, the game was completed in almost complete darkness, during which time the Alliance scored their third goal. A match report in the *Midland Athlete* (24/12/1879) gives a good sense of the farcical last few minutes. "Arthur James sent the ball into the goalkeeper's hands, who, not being able to see, dropped it, and the Alliance scored a third goal. The remaining ten minutes play was carried on in complete darkness." The final score was 5-3 to Unity, ending the Alliance's cup exploits for another season.

Most working men were able to relax with their families over the Christmas break, but for amateur footballers the festive season was a hectic period, with three games in four days. On Boxing Day, the Alliance travelled to Wednesbury for a game against Hall Green Unity, most likely in a six aside tournament, and then on the following day, the club welcomed Stourbridge to Muntz Street. The second XI was just as busy, playing Bordesley Works, and then Stourbridge second team over the same two day period. Then on 29th December, the club members relaxed by playing a match between themselves; Married Players versus Single Players. The event was organised by Mr. Brown, the proprietor of the Red Lion Hotel in Acock's Green, who had prepared a nearby field for the game. The team line ups were:

Married

W. Penfield - Goal
J. Tatton - Back
T. James - Half Backs
G. Smith
G. Penfield
W. Neal - Forwards
A. Wilcox
W. Edden
J. Figures
A. Willetts
F. Holloway

W. Hards and S. Gessey were unavailable for the 'Married' team.

Singles - Player positions not known.

A. Owen
T. Edden
F. James
J. Sparrow
F. Cornforth
Bruff
T. Milnes
H. Clayton
E. Booth
A. James
W. Slater

The fun of the occasion is shown by goalkeeper Billy Edden's choice to play up front, as bragging rights within the club remained equal after a 2-2 draw. A report revealed that "after the game the players and friends sat down to a splendid repast provided by the proprietor of the Red Lion Hotel, and the evening was spent in harmony, songs and recitations were capitally rendered by the players and friends, who returned to Birmingham by the last train perfectly satisfied with the outing."

In the New Year, notable late season victories at Muntz Street included an 11-0 demolition of Smethwick, and an emphatic 6-0 win over St. George's. The Smethwick team was made up of five Alliance second team players, who helped out when the visitors could only muster six of their own.

7.3 MUNTZ STREET'S FIRST FOUR FIGURE CROWD 1880/81

The first major fixture of the 1880/81 season was a thumping 6-1 home win against "the Stoke club" in the first round of the Birmingham Cup. It's interesting that two old friends, Tom Slaney and Fred Hackwood, who, a decade earlier, had been students together at Saltley College, were among the officials. The full line up was:
W. Edden (goal); S.Gessey (back); T. James, F. James and J.Tatton (half backs); W. Slater, A. James (capt.), J.S. Harlow, H. Clayton, W. Rotherham and W. Hards (forwards). Umpires: T.C. Slaney (Stoke) and T. Edden (Alliance). Referee: Mr Hackwood (Wednesbury Old Athletic).

Three weeks later, on 4th December 1880, the club's first ever game against West Bromwich Albion took place at Muntz Street. The Alliance came out on top 2-0, with Tom James scoring one of the goals direct from a corner.

In the Birmingham Cup second round draw held at Nock's Hotel, the Alliance club were given a bye straight through to the third round, and here they received a tough rematch against the same Aston Unity side that had knocked them out in the previous season, courtesy of the dubious Association ruling to order a replay. The Alliance club had felt robbed, but now they had been given almost an immediate opportunity to gain revenge. The Small Heath faithful couldn't wait, and the heightened interest in the game ensured a bumper crowd. The one thousand attendance was the first time a four figure crowd had been seen at Muntz Street, and the team were determined to send them home with a victory. In one of the greatest matches ever seen at Muntz Street, the two teams served up a gripping encounter, with the lead

Arthur James changing hands on three occasions in a ten goal thriller. The scoring sequence went (Alliance first); 1-0, 1-1, 2-1, 2-2, 2-3, 3-3, (half-time 3-3) 4-3, 4-4, 5-4 and 6-4. Six different players scored for the Alliance, including all three James brothers. The final goal, by Arthur James, was a classic. He "made a splendid run nearly the length of the field, passing 4 or 5 men of the Unity, and scoring the sixth goal, amidst loud applause from the spectators."(*The Midland Athlete*, 2nd February 1881).

The momentous 6-4 victory had put the team through to their first quarter-final tie. It was a new experience, especially as it meant playing at a neutral venue for the first time in their history. The Birmingham and District F.A. had decreed that all ties, from the quarter-final stage, were to be played on a neutral ground, with Aston Lower Grounds now the Association's contracted venue. Unlike the earlier rounds, where the gate money was split 50:50 between the competing teams, the money from the quarter final ties was split three ways. Once the Aston Lower Grounds Company had received it's fee, the rest was shared between the two teams and the Association Charity Funds. The draw had pitched the Alliance against the well respected and renowned cup fighters Walsall Swifts, who had retained the Walsall Charity Cup for the past three seasons. The tie, held on 12th February 1881, attracted a respectable, if unspectacular, crowd of one thousand five hundred, each paying a six pence admission charge, and seeing the teams battle out a 2-2 draw. The Alliance were trailing 2-1 when they scored a freak goal to equalise. The Swifts' defender, Alf Jones, described the goal as follows: "We were pressing when the ball was sent by one of the Alliance half-backs well up the field. I was talking to our goalkeeper, some yards from goal, and I ran out to meet the ball with what they call a drop kick in rugby. I met it nicely and it caught the opposing centre-forward on the forehead with so great a force that he dropped like a log, and it was sometime before he came round. Meanwhile the ball rebounded back towards our goal, and although our goalkeeper endeavoured to stop it, it just went over his finger tips, making the score 2-2." (*Walsall Advertiser*, 7th February 1914). The unfortunate Alliance forward was George Goodby. In the replay, held a month later, the Alliance stumbled to a 4-0 defeat, with the Swifts going on to win the cup.

By the time that Walsall Swifts had triumphed in the final on 9th April, by beating Aston Villa 1-0, the Alliance team had already started their cricket season. On the Saturday before the final, the Alliance cricketers had made the short trip to the St. Paul's Road ground in Sparkbrook for a game against the Pickwick club, and on the actual day of the Birmingham Cup Final, they travelled to Perry Barr to play cricket against Perry Athletic. This was the last season in which the Alliance club was able to play cricket matches which overlapped with the tail end of the football season. Competitive football games were now impinging on the previously unchallenged cricket season, with local cup fixtures extending into the whole of April, and on occasions spinning out into May. The new order was gradually taking over.

Alliance cricket team sheets
2nd April 1881 (v. Pickwick) : J. Tatton, Bodenham, Teychenne, Neale, S. Gessey, G. Goodby, Slater, E. Goodby, H. Tatton, Smith, G. Gessey.
9th April 1881 (v. Perry Athletic) : J. Tatton, Bodenham, Teychenne, Neale, G. Goodby, E. Goodby, S. Gessey, Smith, J.S. Harlow, G. Gessey, Parker.

Unsurprisingly, the cricket team comprised of several players from the football team, including John Bodenham, who was Billy Edden's understudy in goal, half-backs Vincent Teychenne and Joseph Tatton, and forwards Bill Slater and John Harlow. Also worthy of note is the appearance of a second Gessey brother, George, who, at twenty years old, was fifteen years younger than his more renowned sibling and team mate, Sam. George Gessey was to make a handful of first team appearances for the club during the 1881/82 football season, playing at the back.

Encroaching into the traditional cricket season wasn't the only impact of the growing number of cup matches. Two other major issues were bubbling away in the background, both linked to the increased football attendances. Firstly, the boost in crowd numbers had only served to emphasise the complete lack of facilities for the watching public, and the terrible conditions they were forced to endure. The experience of watching football was generally an uncomfortable one. Crowds still stood on muddy outfields, with no protection from the elements, either underfoot or overhead. If it rained, the mud would churn up and become as slippery as an ice rink. It's fair to say that the dreadful conditions of football spectators had not been given much consideration by the clubs, but as the crowds gradually increased, the issue could no longer be ignored. Curiously, some progress in this area was briefly referred to in the match report for the Alliance's opening game of the following season (81/82), at Nottingham Forest.

The *Sheffield Daily Telegraph* match report for the game at the Trent Bridge Ground, discloses that "the outskirts of the enclosure were, under new regulations, boarded to protect the feet of spectators". This seems to have been a key turning point in relation to the comfort of spectators, with boarded spectator areas becoming common place at most forward thinking clubs. Naturally, for such "luxury", spectators would have to pay more. So for example, at the Chuckery Ground in Walsall, to stand on a boarded area would cost double that of routine ground admission (i.e. one shilling for boards, and sixpence otherwise).

Wednesbury Old Athletic dealt with the mounting disquiet about their wet and muddy spectator areas by choosing to move grounds. Early in the 1881/82 season, they upped sticks from their Athletic Grounds and started to rent the Wednesbury Oval Ground from one of their rivals, Elwells F.C. Presumably, the cost, or the sheer logistics, of providing boarded areas at their former ground drove their decision. At some enclosed grounds, it wasn't always possible to leave the boards down in between matches.

Was Muntz Street among the early grounds to introduce the new innovation of boarded areas? It's difficult to say, although there is some evidence to suggest not. In December 1882, during the second season of their introduction at some grounds, like Trent Bridge and the Chuckery in Walsall, the abysmal conditions being endured by the Muntz Street faithful were still an issue. An account in the *Midland Athlete* for the game against Spittal reported that "the field was simply slush, from end to end there was not an inch of firm ground, and spectators and players alike were ankle deep in mud." This tends to suggest that Muntz Street was still without boarded areas.

Realistically, it's doubtful that the ordinary Alliance follower would have been willing, or able to afford to pay double the general admission price for the extra comfort, although it is possible that a small section was provided for the more wealthy onlookers. In the 82/83 season, Muntz Street was used as the neutral venue for the Semi-Final of the Wednesbury Charity Cup, Nottingham Forest versus St. George's, perhaps indicating that the ground had been upgraded with a boarded area, enabling it to host the prestigious fixture. As an ambitious club, it is safe to assume that the Alliance would aim to keep pace with this welcome innovation. In an era when most ground improvements would have been carried out by the players themselves, the club wasn't short of volunteers with construction skills. The three Edden brothers earned their living as builders, and although Sam Gessey now worked as an engine fitter at the B.S.A. factory, he had originally been apprenticed as a carpenter. In addition, three of his brothers, John, George and Harry, had now moved to Small Heath to also take up work at the huge B.S.A. factory, where John and George were wire workers, and Harry, like Sam, an engine fitter. They all, no doubt, added to the pool of volunteer labour available to the Alliance.

The other big issue, the increased flow of money into the game from larger crowds, had tempted some clubs to make hidden payments to players, something the Birmingham and District F.A. strongly opposed. Charles Crump, the President, and John Campbell Orr, Treasurer, were both traditionalists who fervently supported the maintenance of the amateur status, where any profits were routinely distributed to local charitable causes. The issue of creeping professionalism would create ripples throughout the football community throughout the early and mid 1880s.

It seems that the Alliance club was firmly in the amateur camp, in line with the local Association's lead. Sam Gessey's allegiance to the club adds weight to this view. It's doubtful whether a sportsman like Gessey, someone with deep amateur roots, would have even considered joining up with the Alliance, if he had any qualms with their ethos. He had known a number of their senior players, including Will Edden and Arthur James, for several years and knew that their sentiments were similar to his own. In Oxford, Gessey had grown up with amateur sport on his doorstep, including contests played on the University Parks grounds by the fiercely amateur student teams, and his own experience of village cricket. Like the founding Alliance players, he was from the old school of sport, where games were played for honour and enjoyment; not for financial reward.

Further proof of the Alliance's adherence to amateur values was exhibited by their continuing generosity to charitable causes. In November 1880 the players had donated £20/1/6d to the Birmingham and Midland Hospital for Women, the proceeds of an earlier home match, "at which the services of the band belonging to the works of Mr. Wright, Garrison Street were given gratuitously."(*Birmingham Daily Post*, 6th November 1880) Mr. Wright's factory, the Universe Works, made ropes and telegraph cables.

Unfortunately, with the influx of gate receipts and the increasing involvement of wealthy factory owners, these traditional amateur values were now in danger. At the Alliance, the old guard of players, and ex-players on the committee, must have felt frustrated as they watched their old values being undermined by increasing outside pressures. The club had been blessed with a sizeable band of faithful one club players, including several from their founding days, whose loyalty was unconditional and not linked to financial reward. The fact that the club was organised and run by the players themselves in the form of a committee, also meant that they were independent and self-governing; in other words free from the interference of any wealthy individuals. Not all clubs in the local Association, however, had remained so tied to the spirit of amateurism, some offering inducements to players, as unfolding events would show.

8
FOOTBALL FEVER IN THE EARLY 1880s

8.1 THE RISE OF JUNIOR FOOTBALL IN SMALL HEATH

The early 1880s saw a huge proliferation of junior football clubs within the Small Heath area, providing a welcome source of young talent for the Alliance to draw on. Players like Harry Morris, who came from Small Heath Alexandra, Billy Figures from St. Andrew's Rovers, and Teddy Hill and Tommy Davenport from Small Heath Royals, all progressed through this route, each going on to feature in the Alliance's storming F.A. Cup run of 1886.

Local junior matches were an ideal grounding for young players, teaching them how to survive the hardened environment of energy sapping pitches and over enthusiastic challenges. Harry Morris, a future captain of the club, knew how to "look after himself" after first learning his football trade on the pitches of Small Heath Park. In 1880 at the age of just fourteen, he and a few friends formed the Small Heath Alexandra club. The physical nature of these early games comes across from comments Harry made when talking in 1916, saying, "We occasionally broke a collar-bone or two.....Yes, we were the boys of the old brigade, if you like. We were a lot of nuts." Among their main rivals were Small Heath Royal, who played at Glover's Lane (now called Road); Small Heath Strollers, formed by the youths from the Sunday Morning School in Wright Street; Villa Cross, who played on Hamstead Road; St. Andrew's Rovers, who played at Hobmoor Lane and Aston Shakespeare based at Aston Cross.

Competition for pitches at Small Heath Park was tight, and Harry used to ensure that his Alexandra club got the best one by carrying the club's goal posts to the park at 6.30 a.m. on match days, and fixing them into the ground before any of his rivals arrived. There were no cross-bars then, just a rope tied to the top of each post. For doing this job, and carrying them back home after the game, he was let off his 3d. weekly sub to the club, which based itself at the local Bijou coffee house. However, the scramble for pitches was getting worse as the number of clubs escalated. After a couple of seasons of jockeying for pitches at Small Heath Park, the Alexandra club managed to find a pitch of their own. It was in Golden Hillock Road, previously used by the B.S.A. works team, but even this was short lived, after they were outbid by another club.

The experiences of the Alexandra club were typical of most clubs who didn't possess their own pitch. Harry complained, "The farmers wouldn't have you unless you paid their price and behaved yourselves." This reference to farmers is revealing, as it not only indicates that the area still had numerous patches of rural enclaves, but also suggests that many games were being played on rough meadow like surfaces. This would naturally have a marked impact on the style of play that was possible. Gradually, the farmers' fields were swallowed up by housing developments, making it even more difficult for clubs to find a home. These early experiences of being pushed from pillar to post in search of a decent pitch seemed to have stayed in Harry's mind. Several years later in 1906, it was Harry Morris, who recommended the acquisition of the disused clay pit on the Coventry Road, which would later become the Small Heath club's St. Andrew's stadium.

Another junior team formed around 1880, the St. Andrew's Sunday School club, never had to worry about laying claim to a pitch. Luckily for them, they had an arrangement to use a field right next to the Small Heath Alliance enclosure. Playing games in the shadow of the Alliance ground was a great encouragement to the many young hopefuls, who surely had aspirations of one day joining up with their Alliance heroes. Alliance officials would often cast their watchful eye over the budding talent, especially Albert Coles the second team secretary/manager. Sam Gessey would also occasionally walk onto the Sunday School pitch to "commandeer" a player or two, if the Alliance team was short of numbers.

One lad who gained his football education in the Sunday School team was another future Alliance captain, the formidable, and impressively named, Caesar Augustus Llewellyn Jenkyns. From the age of fourteen, he spent three seasons (1881-84) in the St. Andrew's Sunday School team, before finally breaking into the Alliance second team. During his spell in the Sunday School team, he built up a fearsome reputation. His large frame and quickness over the ground made him an intimidating sight for opposing forwards, and this combination of speed and weight made him a dangerous customer. His team mates included Frank James, the younger brother of Alliance stars Arthur, Tom and Fred, the goalkeeper Scott Walford, who would later become the secretary and manager of Coventry City F.C., and Alfred Vaughan Jones, a future Alliance first team regular during the 1882/83 season. The Sunday School team's opponents included such teams as Small Heath Dixon Unity, Small Heath Wordesley, West Bromwich Unity, Walsall Lifeboat, Birmingham Standard, Greet Albion, Sparkhill Alliance, St. Silas's, and a Handsworth team called "X,Y,Z".

Vincent Teychenne, a youngster who had first joined the Alliance club during the 1878/79 season without making the first team, decided to drop down for a stint in junior football, as captain of the Wycliffe club. He saw this as the best way of improving his skills, and getting into the Alliance first team. Beginning solely as a cricket club, Wycliffe had originally emerged during the late 1860s, from the school rooms and popular Sunday school at Wycliffe Chapel on the Bristol Road, close to St. Luke's Church. Playing at Calthorpe Park, their cricket opponents included Bathurst, Havelock Unity and Ryland Excelsior. Around 1879, the Chapel also spawned a football team, with St. James' an early opponent. Teychenne flourished during his time at the club, and was soon invited to step up to the Alliance first team for the start of the 1881/1882 season.

8.2 CUP MANIA AT THE ALLIANCE 1881/82

1881/82 was a significant season for the Alliance, as they embraced cup competitions in a big way, by entering four cup tournaments. Alongside their usual appearance in the Birmingham and District F.A. Cup, they made their debut in three other competitions: the F.A. Cup, the Walsall Challenge Cup, and the Wednesbury Charity Cup. It was an exciting time for the players, particularly as they would soon have their first taste of the prestigious F.A. Cup competition. But perhaps the most astounding part of their 1881/82 cup adventures was the fact that they were knocked out of all four competitions by the same team, Wednesbury Old Athletic. The two clubs were now locked into an intense rivalry which had initially been triggered by the Old Athletic's humiliating Birmingham Cup defeat at the hands of the Alliance in 1879/80. It was a rivalry that was to continue for several years, reaching a crescendo in November 1883, after a feisty Walsall Cup tie which resulted in the Alliance angrily resigning from the Walsall and District F.A. More on that later.

Several cup competitions had sprung up in the Midlands during the late 1870s, all seeking to emulate the Birmingham Association's successful model. Among the rival competitions were the Staffordshire Challenge Cup, administered from Stoke, which emerged in 1877/78, and the Licensed Victuallers' Cup in Walsall, introduced a year later by local publicans to raise funds for charities. Perhaps the most intriguing competition, due to the huge size of the trophy and the fact that it was an invitation only event, was the Wednesbury Charity Cup, which started during the 1879/80 season. Earlier that same season, a clutch of three clubs (Aston Villa, Birmingham Cricket & Football Club, and Calthorpe) had become the first teams from Birmingham to enter the F.A. Cup, which had been in existence since 1872. Until now, the Alliance's approach had been quite cautious, only ever committing themselves to the Birmingham Association's cup competition, to avoid overstretching themselves. Entering other competitions incurred additional membership fees for each Association, plus the potential of spiralling travel costs. They would not have wanted to repeat the experience of Aston Villa in 1879/80, who pulled out of an F.A. Cup tie at Oxford University to conserve funds. William McGregor later admitted that it was a "shortage of cash to meet the cost of the journey to Oxford" that had forced Villa to withdraw.

The Alliance's new enthusiasm for cup games coincided with the increased involvement of the Harlow brothers in club affairs. After hanging up their boots at the end of the 1880/81 season, the pair whole-heartedly immersed themselves into serving the club, John as the club's regular umpire, and Peter as club secretary. Significantly, Peter Harlow was the Alliance secretary during the club's surge in cup activity, and must surely take much of the credit for giving the club a new found impetus during this exciting period. In a season overflowing with cup drama, eight cup ties were played in November and December alone. The request to take part in the Wednesbury Charity Cup competition probably caught the Small Heath men a little by surprise. They had already decided to enter three competitions (the F.A.Cup, the Birmingham Cup, and the Walsall Cup), and the invitation from the Wednesbury Charity F.A. risked them being overrun with fixtures. There was no way, though, that they were going to turn down such a flattering request, being one of just twelve clubs invited. The other eleven teams were: Aston Unity, Birmingham Heath, Castle Blues (Shrewsbury), Elwell's (Wednesbury), Oswestry Town, Spital (Chesterfield), St. George's, Wednesbury Old Athletic, Wednesbury Strollers, Wellington, and West Bromwich Albion.

Philip Harlow, the new club secretary, picked up much of his adventurous spirit and willingness to take risks from his father, the notorious secretary of the Birmingham Trades Council, an early day Trades Union organisation, which was often caught up in the rough and tumble of local politics. As secretary of the Trades Council, his father had led a campaign against the Free Trade policy advocated by the town's domineering Liberals. His main concern was that Free Trade, although fine in theory, was constantly being undermined by foreign tariffs on British goods abroad, which was damaging the local manufacturing trade. His brave stance, daring to take on the all powerful Liberals, was to have dire personal consequences. In October 1881, after some ruthless political manoeuvring by the Liberals, he was unceremoniously forced out of his position as secretary of the Birmingham Trades Council, and also expelled as a delegate of the Trades Union Congress. The Alliance duo, Peter and John Harlow, saw all this drama at first hand. They both worked alongside their father in the printing trade and still lived at the family home in Cherrywood Lane. It must have been a difficult time for them, as they watched their father being treated with such disdain.

Despite the political drama surrounding the family, Philip Harlow would have benefited hugely from his father's expertise and guidance during his tenure, as well as acquiring some of his unflinching resolve and spirit. It was no accident that the club made great strides during his stewardship. Being able to learn from his father's experience of networking and operating as the secretary of a high profile organisation in the town was a great encouragement to him. During his regime, having joined the Football Association, the club became sufficiently organised to attend the F.A. general meetings held monthly at the Freemason's Tavern in London, sitting alongside and networking with delegates from the top teams. His networking soon paid off, when he pulled off a notable scoop by fixing up home and away friendly matches against the crack Nottingham Forest club. Until then, Alliance friendly fixtures had been confined entirely to clubs in the local vicinity, either in the Black Country or the Birmingham locality. Now for the first time, they were venturing further a field, signalling their intention to broaden their horizons.

It's no exaggeration to say that the early season fixtures with Nottingham Forest turned out to be among the most significant events in the club's early development. At the time, playing with six forwards, who hunted in pairs, was still the norm locally; two on each wing and two in the centre. The matches with Forest changed all this for the Alliance, as they were introduced to a more progressive style of play with only five forwards. It was a key turning point for the club, as they quickly tried to emulate Forest's example. Without this tactical advancement, it is arguable whether they would have been ready to win their first trophy in the following season. That said, there were plenty of hiccups along the way, and even a three months spell, at the beginning of the following season, when the new approach was temporarily abandoned, only for it to return to favour as the season progressed.

The inventive Forest team had been developing the progressive 2-3-5 formation since the 1878/79 season. Their system encouraged more passing and link play than the usual 2-2-6 formation, with their players positioned more evenly around the pitch. This naturally led to better team work and more tactical play. Contemporary match reports branded the style of football as being more scientific. The man given most credit for this tactical advancement was Forest captain Sam Weller Widdowson, a great football innovator. Already in 1874 he had made his own shin pads, after trimming down a pair of his old cricket pads and tying them to the outside of his socks. Then using the new formation, he had led his team to successive F.A. Cup semi-finals (1879 and 1880), seeing off several top ranked opponents, including the Sheffield club (December 1878), Oxford University (February 1879), and Blackburn Rovers (January 1880), the last by an emphatic 6-0 score line. They were the first working class team to reach this stage of the prestigious competition, and other working class teams like the Alliance were quietly in awe of them.

Visiting the renowned Trent Bridge ground was a definite 'step up' for the Small Heath men. For them it was all part of a valuable learning curve. True to form, the Forest team set up a 3-2 victory by using their cutting edge 2-3-5 formation, as the Alliance men laboured to keep in the game with their more traditional 2-2-6 approach. The result, though, didn't really matter to the Alliance. More important was their first hand experience of the new formation. Forest's impressive team work had been a breath of fresh air to them, and two weeks later, inspired by what they had witnessed, the Alliance team converted to the new 2-3-5 system. By using only five forwards, they were now breaking ranks with most other local clubs, who continued to use the 2-2-6, or similar 1-3-6 formation. It was a bold move to go out on a limb, and experiment with their tactics. Over the coming weeks, they would eventually settle on a 1-1-3-5 formation, with one back, one three-quarter back, three half backs, and five forwards.

Before the Alliance's busy cup campaign began, Arthur James was again on representative duty for the Birmingham Association. He travelled down to the Kennington Oval with the rest of his Association colleagues, to play out a 1-1 draw with the London F.A. team, in a match refereed by Charles Alcock, secretary of the Football Association. Then, a week later, it was into a flurry of cup matches which ran for seven consecutive Saturdays. These games remain the most intensive period of cup matches in the club's history, and there were even more ties to follow later in the season. The incredible sequence started with the club's first foray into the F.A. Cup; a home tie against Derby Town on 5th November. The historic occasion resulted in a resounding 4-1 victory for the Alliance with Bill Slater scoring the club's first F.A.Cup goal.

Throughout November, performances in cup matches continued to go well, with easy wins in both round one of the Birmingham Cup, 7-2 against Aston Clifton, and round one of the Walsall Cup, 3-0 against Aston Unity, interspersed with a creditable 2-2 draw, against Wellington, in round one of the Wednesbury Charity Cup. It was only after the second round F.A. Cup draw, when the Alliance were pitched against their old adversaries, Wednesbury Old Athletic, that fortunes started to change. The Old Athletic team had been waiting two years for a chance to avenge their humiliating Birmingham Cup defeat at the hands of the Small Heath men in 1879, and were fired up for retribution. The memory of that shock defeat still rankled the Wednesbury men, and they weren't about to make the same mistake twice, especially at their own Oval ground in front of three thousand baying spectators.

As if to add to the sense of foreboding, the Alliance team came to the match without their captain and talisman, Arthur James, who was on representative duty in Darwen for an Association match against Lancashire. George Holden, the Old Athletic's star forward, was also away on duty, but his team were able to boast more strength in depth as cover. The Alliance's answer to replacing the absent Arthur James was to move regular half-back, Vincent Teychenne, into the forward line. He could run 100 yards in just over ten seconds, once winning a 25 shillings prize at a local athletics event. His natural speed and sprinting ability were useful assets, but his promotion to the forward line served to highlight the Alliance's lack of options. Nevertheless, he was a great favourite with the home crowd, noted for being able to break down opposition attacks and regain possession with his speedy interceptions. His strength was snuffing out danger with whole hearted challenges and splendid tackling. Playing up front, though, was a different proposition. As it turned out, the match was a complete disaster for the Alliance. Unluckily they lost two men to injury during the game, including the influential Tom James, and struggled to make any impression against the confident Old Athletic sharp shooters, who showed no mercy in front of their jubilant fans. The 6-0 thrashing was a difficult afternoon for young Jack Bodenham in goal, as nine men Alliance were overwhelmed.

By the time the Alliance had restored a semblance of confidence by overcoming Wellington 3-0 in their Wednesbury Charity Cup replay in Shropshire, the club was making plans for a second encounter with the Old Athletics. This time it was the Birmingham Cup which had brought the two clubs together for a swift rematch. Importantly, the Alliance had been given home advantage in the draw, and were determined to turn the tables on their illustrious opponents. It would be the Athletic's first ever visit to Small Heath, and I suspect that they weren't relishing the trip. They knew that the Alliance would be a stiffer proposition on their own turf, with stories of the awful Muntz Street playing surface and the return of Arthur James among their concerns. In front of a one thousand partisan crowd, the two teams served up a thrilling first half as they battled it out in the Muntz Street mud. At half time the game remained evenly poised at 2-2, but in the second half the Old Athletic team again took complete control. The Alliance players seemed to be sapped of energy after a brave attempt to keep their opponents subdued. *The Birmingham Daily Post* commented that "the heavy condition of the ground began to tell on them", as the Alliance team conceded five second half goals in a crushing 7-2 defeat.

The match wasn't the end of the Alliance torment. Unbelievably, in the Walsall Cup second round, the two teams were again drawn to face each other. Alliance hearts must have sunk when they heard the news. Their third cup confrontation in just four weeks took place on the last day of December 1881. By now, it was a deflated Alliance team which trudged over to the Wednesbury Oval for the encounter. Predictably, there was no let up by the impressive Old Athletic side as they clocked up a 5-1 win.

Later in the new year, the two clubs would incredibly be drawn together again; this time in the semi-final of the Wednesbury Charity Cup. Again the Old Athletic team would prevail, although there are no records of the score line.

For most of the season, veteran goalkeeper Billy Edden had been taking a back seat, with second team man Jack Bodenham making a string of appearances. Then on 18th February, Edden reappeared for a friendly against Wednesbury Strollers. Whether this was a pre-arranged decision to give the much loved goalkeeper the opportunity for a deserved send off in front of the Muntz Street faithful, or simply answering an unexpected call to give the battle weary Jack Bodenham a rest, following the string of crushing defeats, we can't be sure. Incredibly, the Muntz Street crowd responded with a terrific attendance of three thousand, nearly three times bigger than the previously recorded best, suggesting that the locals had turned out in their droves to show their appreciation for his great service to the club. The match wasn't played in an amiable spirit though. A report in the *Athletic News* (22nd February 1882) commented that "the game was of a very disorderly nature and high-flown language was indulged in to no small degree, accompanied by various threats of a pugilistic display". In April, Billy Edden made probably his final appearance in a game against Stafford Road Works, when over two thousand spectators flocked to see him for one last time. The size of the crowds show the great esteem in which Billy Edden was held by his adoring public.

One rookie club member who was watching all this adoration from the side was twenty year old William Crisp Rose, who had joined the Alliance club after a spell with Small Heath Rovers. Within two incredible years he would be the England goalkeeper, yet at the Alliance he was never the first choice. With veteran Billy Edden, and Jack Bodenham both ahead of him in the pecking order, young Rose was never given a first team opportunity to show his talent. After starting the 1882/83 season in the second team, he decided to move to Swindon, where he joined the local Swindon club. His time at the Alliance club, though, hadn't been wasted. It seems that Billy Edden's exploits had left a big impression on the young W.C. Rose, who worked hard at Swindon to emulate his hero. Rose would have seen, at close quarters, the techniques and methods used by the experienced Billy Edden at Small Heath, and viewed him as his role model.

W.C. Rose's move to Swindon F.C. led to an almost meteoric rise in his football career. Soon he would be rubbing shoulders with the game's elite, carving out a remarkable football career, first within the southern amateur circles of the London Swifts, and the famous Corinthians club, then to the polar opposite camp of unashamed professionalism at Preston North End. So how did this come about?

Rose's big break came when his goalkeeping exploits at Swindon F.C. were spotted by the secretary of the Wiltshire F.A., William Samuel Bambridge, a man with both a football pedigree and excellent connections within the southern amateur game. An old goalkeeper himself, he had soon recognised Rose's raw talent. Apart from selecting him for the Wiltshire F.A. representative team, he also recommended his new discovery to his old club, the London Swifts, where two of his younger brothers, E.C. and A.L. Bambridge, were prominent players. It was early in the 1883/84 season that W.C. Rose joined up with them. The Bambridge brothers were from another world compared to Rose. Their father was the Royal photographer to Queen Victoria, and another brother, George, was the private secretary to her son, Prince Alfred.
"E.C." was a an insurance clerk at Lloyds , and "A.L." an artist. It must have been quite an ordeal for Rose, an ordinary working class lad and carpenter by trade, who had spent eighteen years of his life around the terraced streets of east Birmingham, to be suddenly mixing with the social elite of Victorian England.

After England call ups in the first British Home Championships in 1884, he was lured up to Preston North End after playing against them for the Corinthians in January 1885. Whether he received any inducements, we can't be sure, but it was almost an unparalleled and controversial move for any player to make. He would have been seen as a traitor by his old amateur team mates and under suspicion of taking illegal payments. A couple of seasons later, his North End career ended in disarray after he went "absent without leave" following the death of his wife, with the North End club claiming that he still owed them money for a loan. He joined Wolves in January 1887, and was a member of their 1893 F.A. Cup winning side.

After his controversial career had ended, it is obvious that he still had a soft spot for his old Small Heath club. In April 1912 he turned out for "Old Heathens" in a charity game at Villa Park, against "Old Villans". He hadn't forgotten his roots.

When Rose began his career with the Alliance club during the 1881/82 season, he had joined at a time when the traditional amateur ethos was gradually coming under threat. After Billy Edden's decision to retire from the team at the end of that season, the only Alliance founders still playing were Fred and Tom James. The so-called "old brigade", players with direct links to the early pioneering days of football in the town, and upholders of the amateur values, were gradually fading from their teams. Those who stayed around as club committee men, or members of the local association, remained staunchly amateur in their outlook, but for the new generation of players, loyalty to the amateur cause was becoming less important. Gradually the pressure towards professionalism was starting to build, as the "old brigade" disappeared from the game. Their old amateur values were now being undermined by payments creeping into the game, most of which were easily hidden, and the growing practice of offering inducements to attract players from outside the area, often from Scotland.

An early season editorial note in the *Midland Athlete* (12th October 1881) made plain it's opposition to professionalism. It read, "Up to the present, football has been a purely amateur sport, indulged in for love of healthy exercise and amusement, and nothing more: and one great reason of its widespread popularity among the masses is the very small capital required to start a club and keep it going. But the very popularity of association football has been the cause of several evils, which will require a strong and determined hand to keep down and prevent ruining the game altogether. Of these evils professionalism is, perhaps, the most dangerous. As far as our information goes at present, we know of no glaring case wherein men have been paid to play football. We use the word glaring, advisedly, for we do know of cases where men have received more than their legitimate expenses to play for a club. But though men are not often paid in cash they are in other ways; it is no uncommon thing for influential members of a club to obtain situations for good players as an inducement for them to play for certain clubs. Then it is not improbable that club funds may or have been used to find a small business for popular players who pose as "mine host" before their admiring club mates. Now this is all very well from one point of view, but can associations allow it to continue? Most assuredly not; and the sooner a law, similar to that which regulates players and gentlemen in cricket, is passed for football the better the game. Men who can afford to give up business for football, who can travel here, there, and everywhere at all times and seasons, men who receive payment for playing in certain matches, men who make a profit out of the game they play, are professionals, and, as such, such not get leave to compete for cups nor take part in Association matches. They play for their livelihood, and ought not therefore to be classed with those who play simply for the honour of winning a cup. Bound up inseparably with this subject is that love of gate money which is fast changing the whole aspect of the game, and that antagonism and hatred between clubs caused by the richer alluring good or promising players from the poorer."

The Birmingham and District F.A. was firmly opposed to professionalism. The president Charles Crump, a founder of Stafford Road Works F.C. and the first captain of the Birmingham Association representative team, was one of the staunchest advocates of amateurism, as were committee men John Campbell Orr and John Carson, both founders of the Calthorpe club (then known as Birmingham Clerks' Association F.C.). The fact that John Carson's first club, Queens Park in Glasgow, had remained ardently opposed to professionalism explains the origins of his stand. Another member of the local Association with strong views was W.H. Jope, a Wednesbury representative. Like many early football men, his interest in amateur sport was much broader than just football. As an active member of the Midland Cross Country Association since 1879, he desperately believed in keeping professionalism at bay across all sports. It was the spirit of sportsmanship which mattered to enthusiasts like him, rather than any financial motivation.

Despite the "old brigade's" loyalty to amateur values, there was no doubt that the move towards professionalism in football was gathering ground. In the Birmingham district there was a suspicion that some clubs were gaining an unfair advantage by giving illegal inducements to attract players. There was speculation in Walsall, for example, that Aston Villa had been breaking the rules by initially making secretive payments to Archie Hunter to journey down from Scotland to play in key matches. By now, the "old brigade" knew that they couldn't stop the inevitable, but they could still slow it down. At the February general meeting of the English F.A. in 1882, held at the Freemason's Tavern in London, it was the Birmingham "old brigade" which had a plan to staunch the flow. Their proposal was:

"That any member of a club receiving remuneration or consideration of any sort above his actual expenses in any match, shall be debarred from taking part in either Cup, Inter-Association, or International contests; and any club employing such a player shall be excluded from the association."

The proposal was put forward by A.E. Daniell of the Calthorpe club, who in 1876 had been a member of the first Birmingham Association representative team, alongside captain Charles Crump. Later, Daniell himself would takeover as captain, with Billy Edden and Arthur James among his association team mates. The seconder was A.W. Mason, also from the Calthorpe club, who coincidentally had been the referee in the F.A. Cup tie between the Alliance and Wednesbury Old Athletic just three months earlier. His time in amateur football stretched right back to the earliest days of the Birmingham Clerks' Association F.C. in 1874, when he played alongside John Campbell Orr and John Carson, both now prominent figures in the Birmingham and District F.A. With ties like these, stretching back over eight years, it is no surprise that they stood shoulder to shoulder in an attempt to halt the rise of professionalism. The basic aim of the Birmingham men's proposal was to limit any player payment to the reimbursement of actual expenses incurred, thereby still outlawing any other rewards or inducements. Unsurprisingly, not everyone supported this stance, particularly the men from Lancashire whose district had seen a number of players arriving from Scotland to play for Lancashire teams. Mr. Hindle from the Lancashire Association wished "a days pay" to be added to the permitted player expenses. Mr. N.L. Jackson, Finchley F.C., proposed to meet this request by inserting the words "and any wages actually lost by such player taking part in any such match" after the word "match" in the original proposal. Dr. Morley, Blackburn Rovers, seconded this, and the proposition , as amended by Mr. Jackson was carried by 47 votes to 17.

In June, at the Birmingham and District F.A. annual dinner and prize giving at the Great Western Hotel, Charles Crump reiterated his wish to keep the game pure. He was confident that the Birmingham district had not been afflicted with professional players, and felt sure that it would never be tolerated. "The great evil, the evil above all others, we need to contend with," he said, "was the betting nuisance." At the same meeting, the players who had represented the local Association during the season, which included Arthur James, were each presented with a gold medal.

Later that summer, at a meeting of the Children's Hospital Managing Committee, a donation of £6 was received from "the Small Heath Alliance Cricket Club"(*Birmingham Daily Post*, 17th August 1882).

8.3 FRANCIS HENRY CRITTALL – AN ALLIANCE MAN FROM 1882, WHO WENT ON TO FAME AND FORTUNE

Francis Crittall joined the Alliance club while he was working at Peyton and Peyton's Bordesley Works in 1882, a leading manufacturer of bedsteads and cycles. A native of Braintree in Essex, his temporary spell in Birmingham had been prompted by his desire to broaden his knowledge of the latest manufacturing techniques, a sortie which turned out to be a great success. On returning to his family's modest ironmongers shop about a year later, he was brimming with new ideas, and in 1884 his Braintree firm became the world's first manufacturer of metal window frames. By the 1920s his business empire, Crittall Windows, had expanded worldwide, with factories in America, South Africa, Australia, New Zealand, India and Germany. Famously his windows were used at the Houses Of Parliament, and on board the Titanic.

He was equally passionate about football, a game he had first experienced in 1874 as a fourteen year old at Chipping Hill School in Witham, near Braintree. His school games were "rough and ready", with no common understanding of the rules. A report for a game against the Standard Club of Colchester noted that "the rules played were their own (Chipping Hill) and not known to their opponents." (*Essex Standard*, 4th December 1874). Soon after leaving school in 1876, Crittall turned out for the first football club to be established in Braintree; Braintree F.C. In his words, the original club "played under mixed rules and a 'go as you please arrangement'. It was a mixture of Rugby and Association, with a little Eton thrown in." In Birmingham, the twenty-one year old Crittall at first gravitated towards the Calthorpe club. His most high profile game came in November 1881, against West Bromwich Albion in round one of the Birmingham Cup. A thousand strong crowd saw his side go down 3-2 at Calthorpe's Bristol Road ground. Later he teamed up for a short spell with the Alliance, the nearest club to his Bordesley Works workplace, playing for the club's second XI. Then, when he returned home to Essex in 1883, he rejoined his local Braintree club.

He was a staunch supporter of the amateur game, a way of thinking which stayed with him throughout his life. In an address to his Crittall factory team, Manor Works F.C., in 1906, he told the assembled players, "You get so beastly conceited, some of you players. You all think that when you get a good club that you are little tin gods on wheels; that you are something superior, and must be bowed down to as idols. In the past we had nothing of that kind; we had no crowd to see us play, and no inducement except for the fun of the thing. I know because I have been through the whole thing. I have played with some of the best clubs in England. When I was in Birmingham I was a member of the Small Heath Alliance, and I played in the first eleven against the best clubs of the day." (*Chelmsford Chronicle*, 27th April 1906). In his 1906 speech, he obviously exaggerated his importance to the Alliance club, as he never broke into the first team, but it's his views on amateurism that are perhaps the most revealing; a throwback in time, and probably similar in sentiment to those held by many of his Small Heath team mates twenty four years earlier. The Alliance second XI team sheet for the game at Walsall White Star on 1st October 1882 was: W.C. Rose (goalkeeper); H. Tatton (back); J. Tatton (capt.), F.H. Crittall and Neale (half backs); Sparrow, Lambert, Goodall, Carter, Owen and Bethall (forwards).

The team sheet shows that veteran forward Joe Sparrow, a founding player, was still active at the club. Incidentally, he was now lodging with the James family at their home in Bordesley Park Road, alongside club mates Arthur and Fred James.

9
THE FIRST TROPHY; A TRIUMPH IN ADVERSITY 1882/83

9.1 REPLACING BILLY EDDEN

As the 1882/83 season began, the Alliance club was still adjusting to the retirement of Billy Edden, one of club's greatest players. By chance, his retirement had coincided with the introduction of a new law which now made wooden cross-bars compulsory.

Billy Edden in February 1881

He had been the first choice goalkeeper since the historic first match against Holte in November 1875, and had remained more or less a permanent fixture ever since. Billy Edden's name was synonymous with the Alliance club, not only as a loyal player, but also as one of the main architects of it's formation, and a past secretary. His absence from the team sheet was a big loss. Quite literally he had always been there. Never before had the club's committee even had to think about who would be playing in goal. Now, after seven seasons, time had caught up with him. Goalkeeping was a young persons' game and at the age of thirty-one, it was becoming more difficult for Billy's body to recover from the knocks and bruises. Goalkeepers could still be charged by opposing players even when the ball was nowhere near, and they were often the target of premeditated physical assault. With six forwards the norm, one was usually deployed exclusively to stand by the goalkeeper and make his life a misery. As soon as the ball was sent towards the goal, it was his job to clatter into the goalkeeper like a "bull at a gate". Forwards would not only measure their success by the number of goals scored, but also by the number of times they could get the goalkeeper "through the goal posts". Doing both at the same time would be considered a bonus. Quite simply there was no protection offered to goalkeepers. The best goalkeepers, like Billy, soon learned how to protect themselves. One tactic was to lower the shoulder as the attacker charged, and "pitch-fork" him, as it was termed, over his head. This was a highly dangerous manoeuvre for the forward, and shows that the aggression was not all one sided.

Replacing Billy Edden was never going to be easy. The original plan had been for John "Jack" Bodenham, the twenty-two year old second team keeper, to step seamlessly into his shoes, but this was before his confidence had been dented by the avalanche of goals he had conceded against the rampant Wednesbury Old Athletic team during the previous season's cup sagas. After this, the Alliance committee had seemingly lost faith in him, and decided to go for a new man. The man drafted in was "Archie" Vale, who had been making a name for himself at the nearby St. Luke's club, having previously risen through the ranks of the local football scene. His first known club, as recalled in 1916 by George Jenks the former Excelsior club goalkeeper, was Ellen Street Victoria. Ellen Street is situated just south of the old Hockley railway station (now called the Jewellery Quarter station), although George remembered them using a pitch two and a half miles away, at Cannon Hill Park.

By 1880/81, "Archie" had progressed to the more senior St. Luke's club, where he was given the opportunity to play in early rounds of the Birmingham Cup, his first competitive games. Trying to discover his precise identity has proved frustrating. No-one called Archie or Archibald Vale, even as a second name, is recorded as being born in the U.K. during the 1850s or 1860s, which only serves to deepen the mystery. Clearly "Archie", as he was called in contemporary reports, was just his nickname, making it almost impossible to track him down. There were a couple of other local players with the Vale surname, brothers Charles and William Vale, but neither of them could feasibly be "Archie". The two lived at their father's pub, the Crown Inn in Villa Street, Hockley. Charles Vale, of the Perry Athletic club, actually played against "Archie" of St. Luke's, when the two clubs met in the Birmingham Cup in November 1881, and the other brother, William Vale, was secretary of the Handsworth Oakfield club.

Tom and Fred James were now the last of the founding players still playing, both holding down regular places in the team as half backs, usually alongside the youthful Vincent Teychenne. As the new season opened, all three James brothers were still key players in the team. The influential Arthur had been captain since the 1877/78 season and was still considered the Alliance's most prized asset. Billy Edden continued working behind the scenes, helping with training sessions, and his younger brother Tom, still involved, replaced John Harlow as the club's regular umpire.

9.2 NEW BLOOD FROM POTTER'S FIELD

The opening game of the season was a goalless draw at Camphill, the new home of Aston Unity. They had recently been displaced from the Lower Grounds meadow after just one season in a sign of their slip down the pecking order. The Camphill ground was normally home to Pickwick Cricket Club, and curiously the Unity, and

Alliance football teams were left hanging around, waiting for Pickwick to complete their game of cricket before they could get on with their match.

In a seemingly retrograde step, the Alliance team was back to their old 2-2-6 formation. Whether it was a knee jerk reaction to last season's mixed results, or simply a pragmatic way of accommodating the surfeit of promising young forwards now on their books, we don't know. It would have been perfectly understandable for the club to have doubts about persevering with the new system, especially as they were out on a limb, with most other local clubs not following suit. It's more likely, though, that Arthur James wanted to give opportunities to some newly arrived forwards, the most promising being Tommy Green and Eddie Stanley, both quick and skilful. Reverting back to six up front would help to fit them in the team, alongside the powerful combination of Wally Jones, Walter Hards, Bill Slater and Arthur James himself.

Newcomers Tommy Green and Eddie Stanley had spent their football apprenticeships on the free open spaces of Potter's Fields, an area of old farmland adjoining Aston Park, once farmed by the Potter family. Although Richard Potter, the last incumbent, had moved away over two decades earlier, the flat meadows were still affectionately known by the locals as Potter's Fields. The farming Potter family had left in 1858 when Aston Park, including their 250 acre farm, had moved into public ownership. Now the vacant fields had become a magnet to the plethora of junior teams in the district, and it didn't cost a penny to use them.

It was at Potter's Field, during the 1879/80 season, that Tommy Green had first built his reputation as a fearless marauding forward of the old school type, roughing up goalkeepers and terrorising defenders. His team was Dreadnought F.C., and one of their biggest weekly struggles, like many others using Potter's Fields, was to commandeer a decent pitch. Each week, someone in the team would need to carry their "goal sticks" to the fields, and stake out a claim for a pitch. The Dreadnought captain was J. Green, perhaps Tommy's brother or cousin. Much of Tommy's early life remains a mystery. In a retrospective article, dated 15th January 1915, the *Sports Argus* confidently referred to Tommy Green as "a famous Birmingham born forward", although some modern on-line player listings give Worcester as his birthplace. Whatever the truth, it was his impressive displays for Dreadnought F.C. on Potter's Fields, that first brought him to the attention of several senior clubs in the district. His choice was to join the nearby St. George's club, where for two seasons, 1880/81 and 1881/82, he seemed well settled, playing alongside his pal Dennis Hodgetts. But then things changed. Out of the blue, he teamed up with Small Heath Alliance for the start of the 1882/83 season. Had he fallen out with St. George's? It certainly seemed a hasty move, and barely four months later he had moved again, this time for a short spell at Aston Unity, raising suspicions that he was playing 'fast and loose' in an effort to solicit a more lucrative deal. It was perhaps his move to

Lancashire, in September 1883, that gave the clearest evidence of his true motivation; money. After turning up for a stint at Great Lever in Bolton, it was obvious that a deal involving some form of incentives had been struck. Remember that this was a couple of years before professionalism was legalised. Cynically, it could be said that Tommy was ahead of his time. He knew that he had a value, and was happy to be treated as a commodity. He was an early day mercenary, seeking to make a fast buck wherever he could. He was also joined in Lancashire by his old pal from his St. George's days, Dennis Hodgetts. Later, Alliance stalwart Harry Morris would comment that "Tommy Green and Dennis Hodgetts were not particular for whom they played so long as they got 10 shillings and sixpence cab fare." He suggested that the term "cab fare" covered a multitude of sins during the pre-professional days, indicating that it was a euphemism for an illegal payment. The episode certainly shows that the pair were not at all bothered about club loyalty.

Eddie Stanley's career was completely different; the model of a loyal club servant. Once he had joined Small Heath Alliance, he never went anywhere else, becoming one of their greatest ever players. He had originally picked up the game at Adderley Park, just a street away from his childhood home in Highfield Road. The renowned Saltley College team which played close by, was one of Eddie's earliest football influences, but it was at Potter's Fields in Aston where he really made his name and raised his standing. In his teens, he would walk the two miles, or so, to Potter's Fields, soon linking up with Clyde F.C., a short lived club based at the Upper Grounds Hotel, next to Aston Park. By coincidence, the Clyde F.C. team of 1879/80 also included another future Alliance player, defender Richard Elliman. Both joined up with the Small Heath outfit ready for the 1882/83 season.

9.3 THE FIRST PLAYER TO TURN OUT FOR BOTH THE ALLIANCE AND ASTON VILLA

For the second year running, it was the revered Forest team who visited Small Heath for the opening home game of the season, a reflection of the cordial relations between both clubs. Making their Alliance debuts for the Alliance that day were fellow Welshmen and pals, W. Roberts, and the diminutive John Jones, who paired up on the left hand side of the forward line. Roberts had recently moved down from Ruabon in North Wales, where he had been a member of the Druid's club. Three weeks later, he unwittingly made football history in the town by becoming the first player to represent both Small Heath Alliance and Aston Villa, when he made his Villa debut against Sheffield Wednesday at Perry Barr. Clearly no rivalry existed between the two clubs during this early amateur period, and it's hardly surprising that Roberts' achievement has, until now, remained undiscovered. As it happened, Roberts' Villa career turned out to be hugely successful, twice winning the Birmingham Association Cup, in 1883 and 1884, and the Mayor of Birmingham Charity Cup in 1883.

Later in the season, between Christmas and the New Year, Roberts made a second appearance for the Alliance in a game versus Spital of Chesterfield. Now a regular in the Villa team, he once again played alongside his pal John Jones, this time in defence. The *Athlete* journal reported that "the two Welshmen prevented any score" and "worked well together at the back." The account also said that with Bill Slater absent, "Roberts of the Villa, more than filled the vacancy, as he stopped some very dangerous runs while playing back in the first half, and in the second made spectators forget the rain by his amusing tricks in his old position, left forward." The match finished 3-0 to the Alliance.

9.4 SHOCKING EVENTS AT RUABON

The 1882/83 season would signal the Alliance's intent to spread their name and influence further a field. Their growing self confidence and ambition now saw them set up fixtures in more distant locations, including North Wales, the Potteries, and Lancashire.

The early season game in North Wales was the Alliance's longest trip so far, as the team journeyed to Ruabon, a small town just south of Wrexham, to face the Druids. The players needed an early start for the laborious rail trip which took them via Wolverhampton and Shrewsbury. Until now fixtures had been more localised, avoiding the need for such long distance and expensive trips, but times were quickly changing and the Alliance team was getting more adventurous. One Alliance player who was already accustomed to travelling around the country was Arthur James, a regular in the Birmingham and District F.A. representative team. He had routinely played in games as far a field as Glasgow, London, Sheffield, and Darwen in Lancashire. The furthest any of his team mates had gone was to towns in the Midlands, such as Nottingham, Derby and Wellington. The arduous trip to North Wales was a new experience for them. It was a journey, however, that would have serious repercussions for club. The match was to leave captain Arthur James gravely injured and his career in jeopardy. So what happened? The following letter, which appeared in the *Wrexham Advertiser* on Saturday 18th November 1882, four weeks after the match, gives a good insight into the nature of injuries to Arthur and the strong feelings it aroused.

'Sir, Under the heading "Table Talk", the Birmingham Daily Mail on Saturday, an evening paper, has the following paragraph :
"One of the most prominent football players - Arthur James of the Small Heath Alliance - an exceedingly fast and clever forward, who has played in some of the best matches in which the Birmingham Association has been engaged - has been at death's door during the present week from the effects of an accident sustained in a recent match with the 'Druids' in Wales. James was knocked about so badly in the course of the game that he has since been confined to his bed by a complication of internal

disorders, and on Wednesday the physician attending him gave little, if any, hope of his recovery. Yesterday it was reported that he had succumbed to his injuries, and a gentleman, prominently identified with the Birmingham Football Association wrote a feeling letter to the secretary of the club condoling with them on the unfortunate loss they had sustained. Happily, the report of James' death proves to be unfounded. His condition last night was said to be much improved, and though he will probably recover, his football days are at an end for a long time to come." Now I think I am correct in saying that the Druids were ever notorious for their exceedingly rough "horse play", and I also feel sure it was due in great measure to this that so much party feeling was shown when the Druids played any of their cup ties at Wrexham. The Druids should remember they are, by virtue of their occupations, physically stronger than the majority of opponents they meet, and they should therefore, exercise a little more discretion in their charging. The game of football does not consist of indiscriminate charging and knocking your opponents all over the place, but rather a rapid movement and discreet passing of the ball with an endeavour to avoid charging at all. I write this with all deference to the Druids, but I think they will admit that the publication of such paragraphs as the above seriously tends to bring into disrepute both their own and other Welsh clubs, and I hope it will be the means of making them a little more forbearing in any future matches they play. -
    Yours R.'

The issue of rough play and charging into opponents had been a bone of contention within football circles for several years. Tripping and hacking was completely outlawed, and the use of hands to hold or push opponents was also outside the laws of play. However it was an accepted practice to charge into a player who had possession of the ball, and there didn't seem to be any clear line between a fair charge, and what was considered reckless or foul play. The tactic of charging was often used purely to intimidate a more skilful opponent, and it was usually the tricky, clever players who came in for the most stick. Serious injury and even death occurred at worryingly regular intervals.

One such example was the case of twenty year old Herbert Dockerty, an apprentice leather finisher, who died following a reckless charge playing for Ashby de la Zouch against Coalville in February 1878. It was a notorious case as his assailant, William Bradshaw, was committed for trial at Leicester Assizes for manslaughter. The court heard that as Dockerty was dribbling with the ball, Bradshaw ran towards him to charge him. Seeing him approaching, Dockerty kicked the ball past him, only to be clattered by a flying leap from Bradshaw, who was completely off the ground with his knees up, catching Dockerty in the stomach. The judge, Lord Justice Bramwell said it would be safer to consider, in spite of some evidence to the contrary, that the accused was playing in accordance with the rules of the game. Acting on the spirit of these directions, the jury returned a verdict of "not guilty" of manslaughter. The jury did however suggest a recommendation that the laws of football should be altered.

They could not understand how such an obviously unfair challenge was not considered "a foul".

At an earlier sitting of the coroner's court the tragic last few hours of Herbert Dockerty's life were described by his sister. With her assistance, he had managed in great pain to get home and was put to bed. A doctor was called to his home, where he lived with his widowed mother, but could do little to save him. He died the following afternoon, the cause being the rupture of his intestines. Apparently his last words to his sister were "Forgive Bradshaw, all of you as I forgive him." The tragic accident not only resulted in a pointless death of a young man in his prime, but also left behind a shocked and distraught family. Needless to say the football authorities did not alter the laws of the game as suggested by the jury.

Back at Small Heath, the serious injury to Arthur James had been a shocking blow to his team mates, particularly his brothers Tom and Fred. The pair must have been in a terrible state after the game as they helped Arthur to negotiate the long rail journey home from North Wales, uncertain about the extent of his internal injuries. Every jolt of the carriage would have caused him pain and discomfort. The morale of the team was being severely tested, but their spirit remained unbroken. Bill Slater, a centre forward who had joined from St. Luke's at the start of the 1880/81 season, was asked to stand in as captain for the distraught team, as Arthur lay in his sick bed, at his home in Bordesley Park Road.

On the Saturday following the Druid's match, Bill Slater led the troubled team to a heart warming 13-1 home win against Elwell's F.C., a works team from the Elwell's foundry in Wednesbury. The players had done Arthur proud, turning on the style for their stricken captain, hoping to raise his spirits. But things weren't looking good for him. As he lay prostrate, being nursed by his mother and sixteen year old sister, Matilda, his condition reportedly deteriorated. There was no National Health Service to support the James' family, and the household was extremely crowded by today's standards. As well as his parents, seven of Arthur's brothers and sisters were crammed into the house, their ages ranging from his twenty-two year old team mate, Fred to seven year old Eleanor. Everyone was on edge about his condition, including the men at the local Association. The Birmingham F.A. had quickly been notified of his plight, as he had originally been selected to represent them at Bramall Lane, against the Sheffield F.A. team, on the Saturday following the Druid's game.

Rumours were also flying around that the club might scratch from their scheduled F.A. Cup first round match on 4th November, at home to Stafford Road Works in what was only their second ever F.A.Cup campaign. However the team was determined to carry on as normal, even though twenty-five year old Arthur was still gravely ill. Undaunted, Bill Slater led the team out at Muntz Street where they bravely battled to a creditable 3-3 draw, with both Tom and Fred James amongst the scorers. Understandably though, the emotion and turmoil of the previous two weeks was bound to catch up with the team, and in the next two games the club stumbled out of two cup competitions. Firstly, on 11th November, they narrowly slipped out of the Birmingham Cup with a 1-0 defeat at the Chuckery ground, against Walsall Town, the holders of the Staffordshire Cup. Then, a week later, Stafford Road Works knocked them out of the F.A.Cup in the first round replay.

Although these early cup exits were disappointing, the biggest achievement had been for the club to keep going and complete their fixtures during this emotionally charged period. The team had shown commendable resilience and fighting spirit at a time of great adversity. What's more, later that season, still without Arthur James, the team was to surprise all observers and show true fighting spirit by winning their first ever trophy. The plucky Alliance team would go all the way in the Walsall and District F.A. Charity Cup.

9.5 THE VICTORIOUS WALSALL CUP CAMPAIGN 1882/83

The Walsall Cup was one of the earliest local cup competitions, starting in the 1878/79 season soon after the formation of the Walsall and District F.A. For the first three years it was known as the Walsall Licensed Victuallers' Cup due to the sponsorship given by several Walsall publicans. The original cup became the property of Walsall Swifts after they had won it three years in a row, 1878/9, 1879/80 and 1880/81. They then won for a fourth year running, in 1881/82 after a new cup, now called the Walsall and District F.A. Charity Cup, was purchased for the competition.

The Alliance club was one of twenty five to enter the 1882/83 competition, their triumphant campaign beginning with a round one bye. In round two they were paired with Pelsall Rovers, a team from a mining village on the Bloxwich Road near to Walsall, who had a reputation for "unnecessary roughness", typical of many unskilled village teams of the period. Their players were predominantly miners, colliery workers and iron workers. Some worked as "puddlers", hard manual work in sweltering conditions, using furnaces to turn the raw pig iron into usable wrought iron. Despite Pelsall's rustic and physical approach, the Alliance brushed them aside with a 3-0 victory, to set up a third round tie against Darlastan All Saints, who had beaten Frederick Street Works of Walsall 13-1 in the previous round.

Away from the Walsall Cup campaign, the Alliance club had organised an intriguing Boxing Day fixture, playing host to the renown Accrington club from Lancashire. The match was the first day of the Lancashire club's three day Christmas tour of the Midlands, which scheduled two matches in Birmingham and one in Nottingham. It was now fashionable for prominent clubs to fix up a programme of matches in another football hotbed, to test out their standing, and enjoy the accompanying social side of the trip. The Accrington party had travelled down to Small Heath on the morning of the match, with almost inevitably two players missing the train. The ruffled pair managed to get a later train, only to arrive as the game was ending, with Accrington victorious by a 3-0 score line. For the match, the Alliance team had returned to their progressive 2-3-5 formation, something they had abandoned at the end of the previous season. It was a forward thinking decision by the stand in captain, Bill Slater, and although his team was outmanoeuvred by the excellent passing game of Accrington, their defeat wasn't blamed on the change in team formation. They had simply met a better team.

On the following day, Accrington kept up their good form by defeating Aston Unity 5-2. Interestingly, the game was played at the Villa ground in Perry Barr, instead of Unity's usual Trinity Road home. Villa were due to tour Lancashire in early February, and it was reported that several Villa players were among the crowd to see how Lancashire football was developing. On Accrington's final day, 28th December, they made the trip from Birmingham to Nottingham, only to find that their planned match with Notts County had been called off due to the field being flooded. The first the Accrington players knew of their plight was when they read a poster stuck to the wall outside the ground. The Notts County club hadn't even tried to warn them beforehand, and they were furious. This brief account of the three day tour gives a good sense of the laborious effort needed to complete such a punishing schedule. Three games in three days, including travel to and from Lancashire was no picnic, but shows how driven the players were.

In late January 1883, the Alliance returned to action in the Walsall Cup. Their third round tie against Darlaston All Saints provided a notable landmark, as the club clocked up it's biggest ever competitive win, 16-0, against a fragile All Saints team. The thumping victory was not all down to the good play of the Small Heath men, though. The town of Darlaston had been reeling from a lingering outbreak of smallpox, and with morale low, the football club had only been able to muster eight players for the game. The outbreak had been ongoing since September 1882, and the Darlaston Local Board had been desperately trying to prevent it's spread by setting up a new isolation hospital in the town. It had been reported that in Walsall, just three miles away, another hospital was full to the brim with forty-five cases of smallpox. Although vaccinations of a sort existed in the form of lymph direct from the blood of calves, it was not widely available in the Midlands, and in any case, beyond the means of most working people.

Against this background, it is a testament to the spirit of the eight Darlaston men who bravely turned out to face the impossible odds stacked against them. It would have been easy for them to simply duck out of the fixture, but they showed tremendous backbone in difficult circumstances. After arriving late, the officials immediately decided to reduce the game to one hour's duration, so that the match could be finished before sunset. Kicking off at 4 p.m. in front of two hundred spectators, the plucky All Saints men kept the score to 6-0 at half-time (30 minutes), but as their eight players tired on a "wretched pitch", they conceded a further ten in the second half, the game ending 16-0. The curtailment of the game to just one hour was a blessing for the All Saints team, rescuing them from further punishment.

The crushing victory set up an altogether sterner test in the semi-final, against a strong St George's team from Aston. St George's had built a solid reputation, and later in the season would go on to win the Staffordshire Cup by beating West Bromwich Albion 2-1 at the Stoke ground. They also boasted a couple of regulars from the Birmingham F.A. representative team, goalkeeper Harry Stansbie and left winger Dennis Hodgetts.

A few weeks before the semi-final, the Alliance had suffered a major injury scare when their stand in captain, Bill Slater, badly twisted his ankle. His injury, coming on top of Arthur James' prolonged absence, was a major blow. Would he be fit for the big game, which was only three weeks away? It was touch and go. The injury seems to have happened during the friendly against Wednesbury Old Athletic, a match cut short by farcical conditions. *The Athlete* journal reported, "The rain fell in torrents the whole time, and for hours before the match, yet the wet overhead was not nearly so objectionable as the sea of mud and water that covered the ground (Muntz Street), and between the ridges, rivers of water traversed the field." These ridges were a notorious feature of the Alliance playing surface, jokingly called the "celery trenches" by supporters. An idea of their size is given in the following extract from the same match report, which describes the scene after Sam Gessey had fallen after heading the ball. It says, "He appeared to have made his couch in a soft and sloppy hollow between the ridges". In other words the folds in the ridges were big enough for someone to lie in. The scale of the ridges tends to suggest that they were a legacy of the field's previous agricultural use. With undulations like this, it is hardly surprising that Bill Slater managed to twist his ankle.

In a race to get him fit for the semi-final, he was rested from the next two games, Walsall Swifts and Saltley College, as anxious club mates held their breath. In truth though, it was never likely that the stand in captain would miss the semi-final, even if his ankle was still troublesome. He was such a vital figure to the team that he would be prepared to play at all costs. Resolutely, he led his team out to face St. George's at Villa's Wellington Road enclosure at Perry Barr, the neutral venue chosen by the Walsall F.A. It was the first time that the Small Heath club had played on Villa's ground, which at the time was fairly ramshackle. The top goal stood upon a hillock, and there was a pool in one corner behind the enclosure, an area called "lone corner". A disappointing crowd of around 700 spectators was blamed on the "sixpenny gate".

As expected, the match wasn't easy for Slater. One report observed, "Slater, not in his best form, his ankle being twisted some weeks back, no doubt made a difference to his usual accurate centring." Nevertheless, he gamely stuck to his task and it was one flash of first half cleverness from the brave captain that swung the game, when he put in a perfect cross for Charlie Knowles to sweetly head home. The single goal was enough to put the Small Heath men through to their first ever final, fully vindicating Slater's decision to play. Mind you, Slater hadn't done his ankle any favours, and he was forced to sit out the next match against Walsall Town. He didn't really care. All that mattered was that the Alliance had booked their place in the Walsall Cup Final.

Throughout the finely balanced semi-final, a key feature of the Alliance performance had been the expert half-back play of Tom and Fred James. In particular, Fred James completely snuffed out the threat of Dennis Hodgetts on the left wing, never giving him any freedom to show off his skills in the tightly fought match.

In the other semi-final, Wednesbury Old Athletic beat the holders Walsall Swifts 3-2, their first defeat in the competition, after holding the trophy for four successive years since its inception. So the stage was all set for the Alliance to face their old adversaries Wednesbury Old Athletic in the final: a daunting prospect. In the previous season, Old Athletic had easily dumped them out of four separate cup competitions, including a 6-0 win in the F.A. Cup and a 7-2 win in the Birmingham Cup. The pundits were completely discounting the Alliance's chances, even though they had recently beaten their opponents 4-1 in a friendly. This had been casually dismissed as a 'blip' caused by the atrocious conditions. The Alliance men had other ideas and were not easily fazed by such talk.

Speculation was rife that Arthur James could possibly be fit for the final. He had been spotted "on the meadow", as the Muntz Street ground was sometimes called, taking shots at goal and testing out his fitness. Commentators in Walsall were no doubt keen to promote this story in a bid to boost crowd numbers, but privately Arthur James had already told his team mates that he wouldn't be making his comeback in the final, loathe to deprive any of them of a medal opportunity.

The Walsall Cup Final was a big occasion in the Midland's football calendar, attracting a crowd of four thousand to the Chuckery ground in Walsall. The Old Athletic team were used to big matches, having already appeared in several local finals, including the Birmingham and District F.A. Cup Final in 1877 and 1879, the Staffordshire Cup Final in 1880, and the Wednesbury Charity Cup Final in 1881 and 1882. For the Alliance team however, it was a completely new experience; their first ever final. It was clear from the outset that the Old Athletic team planned to exploit this inexperience, and give the Alliance players no time to settle. Furthermore, having won the toss, the Old Athletic captain George Holden, asked the Alliance team to play against the wind, and with the low sun glaring into their eyes.

From the kick off, the Old Athletic went straight at the Alliance, playing at a fast pace and trying to dominate their less experienced opponents. Their intention was to stamp their authority on the game and get early goals. They had opted to play with six forwards, hoping to intimidate and overrun the Alliance defence. The well drilled Alliance back division had other ideas. After withstanding the initial onslaught, it was the Alliance who started to get on top. Their solid team work and good passing began to tell, as they hit back. In a blistering thirty minute spell they took complete control of the game, scoring four goals, as the Old Athletic game plan completely unravelled. The Alliance forwards made run after run, in a performance that completely stunned the Old Athletic team.

The *Midland Athlete* match report described the goals as follows:

Goal 1: "After combined action between Jones, Hards and Knowles, and a well judged return by Tom James to the right wing, Stanley secured the first goal."

Goal 2: "From a well judged pass by Whitehead, Knowles and Hards got well down the left, and after a lot of close passing between Jones, Stanley and Slater, Knowles put the finishing touch to goal number two."

Goal 3: "W. Jones changed the venue of play with a grand close dribble halfway down, and then Knowles took up the run, and centred splendidly, although Jack Holden was bothering him not a little. Hards passed to W. Jones, who put in a hot 'un, which Kent (the Old Athletic's goalkeeper) repelled; but Whitehead smartly returned, and Slater sent a beauty low down from the right which Jones assisted through."

Goal 4: "Knowles and Hards gained a cheer upon passing the whole Wednesbury rear rank very cleverly, and Stanley, with a well gauged shot, gained goal number four for Small Heath."

Even with a 4-0 half-time lead, the Alliance were in no mood to risk their advantage, and Slater decided to strengthen his back division by moving Knowles from the forward line. "With only four forwards at work, strange to say, the Small Heath men kept their opponents' backs and goalkeeper at it hard and fast, their accurate passing and close dribbling being a treat to witness," commented the *Midland Athlete* report. In the dying minutes, Old Athletic pulled a goal back through Wood, but this didn't take any of the gloss of a famous victory. Against the odds, the Alliance had pulled off one of their greatest triumphs, thumping the red hot favourites 4-1. The performance of Eddie Stanley, with two goals and two assists, gave him a justifiable claim for man of the match. He had only made his Alliance debut six months earlier, but already the twenty-two year old, Saltley born forward, had become an indispensable member of the team, such was his impact. Although he was christened Albert Stanley with no middle name, he was always known as "Eddie" at the Alliance, where he stayed for nearly a decade.

The dreadful injury to Arthur James earlier in the season seems to have been a major motivating force for the players, inspiring them to a terrific victory. It should also be remembered that the Alliance's expert use of the 2-3-5 formation had given them a complete tactical domination of the game. By persevering with the system since Christmas, Slater's men were now completely at ease with it, not only enabling them repel the Old Athletic forwards, but also to completely outplay and outmanoeuvre the Wednesbury men across the whole pitch. It was a tactical triumph for the Alliance, and in particular Bill Slater, who had taken the risk to re-establish the 2-3-5 system within the team. An interesting question is whether the team would have deployed it if Arthur James had remained fit? At the start of the season, before his serious injury, his instinct had been to go back to 2-2-6, a system he had used throughout his career, both for the Alliance and on representative duty for the Birmingham Association. Perhaps he had found 2-3-5 too radical a step, and wanted to revert back to what he knew best. We'll never know for sure, but it is possible that he would have preferred to retain the more old fashioned approach of six forwards.

The day of the Alliance's Walsall Cup Final triumph was also the day of the F.A. Cup Final at the Kennington Oval in London. That match was refereed by Charles Crump, founding member and president of the Birmingham F.A. and now a member of the F.A. Council. At the end of the game, after the players had washed and changed, the F.A. Cup was given to the victorious Blackburn Olympic team on the pitch, the first time that it had been handed out in this way. Previously it had always been presented at a private dinner, usually several weeks later. The Alliance team received their cup, the Walsall F.A. Challenge Cup, in the more traditional way. Over a month after their Final, after the season had ended, a formal presentation was held at the Priory Hotel in Walsall on 7th May 1883. Following a celebratory dinner, the cup was handed over to Bill Slater the captain, and each member of the team given a winners medal.

Three weeks before picking up the Walsall Cup, Bill Slater had taken his team to the rising hotbed of football in Lancashire to play Accrington. It was the club's first visit to Lancashire and received a lot of press interest, both locally and nationwide, billed as a contest between the winners of the Walsall Charity Cup and the second holders of the Lancashire Cup, Accrington. Disappointingly, the end of season foray ended in a resounding 4-1 defeat. It seems, with several regulars not making the trip, that the match in Lancashire was one game too many for the Alliance players. They had performed heroically throughout their trophy winning run, but the euphoria was now fading as the strain of a draining season, including ongoing concerns about the future of their talisman Arthur James, started to take it's toll. Of the founding players still involved in the team, Fred James was as reliable as ever, playing in his usual position in the half back line, but his brother Tom didn't make the trip. Another founder, Tom Edden, who had retired as a player at the end of the previous season, made the trip to act as an umpire.

Winning the Walsall Cup had inevitably thrust the victorious Alliance players into the local spotlight. Goalkeeper "Archie" Vale, who conceded only one goal throughout the entire cup campaign, was now wanted by the Aston Villa club. They had won the Birmingham Cup for three of the last four seasons to dominate the local football scene, and it was only natural for players to be flattered by their interest. Vale was no different, lured over to the Perry Barr outfit for the start of the 1883/84 season, and becoming the second player, after W. Roberts, to play for both Villa and Blues. It wasn't all plain sailing for Archie at Villa, though, as he never managed to fully establish himself as their number one. He made intermittent appearances throughout the 83/84 season, before being consigned to the Villa second team during 84/85. Perhaps his biggest game for Villa was an F.A. Cup tie at Queen's Park, Glasgow in January 1884, in which Villa went down 6-1 in front of a 10,000 crowd. The press (*Morning Post*, 21st January 1884) reported that the crowd included 1,200 "excursionists from Birmingham", perhaps one of the earliest examples of mass away travel.

10
THE ALLIANCE STRIVE TO KEEP PACE
1883 TO 1885

10.1 A NEW BREED OF ADMINISTRATOR

Until 1883, the key post of honorary secretary was filled by a current team member, or an ex-player. Part of the enjoyment for these amateur players was to be able to run their own club, and it was only natural that they preferred to keep control within their own ranks. By paying in their weekly subscriptions, they automatically became members of the club and eligible for election onto the controlling committee. Details of the administrative arrangements for the first couple of seasons aren't known, but it is believed that the bulk of the work was done by Billy Edmonds, and Tom James. Then between 1877 and 1882, other players, such as Billy Edden and Philip Harlow, stepped up.

During the early 1880s, the club started to attract more and more non-playing members, as it became a social focal point, not just for the players, but also for many local residents and businessmen who had an allegiance to the club. One such businessman who joined the committee during this period was Alfred Ansell, the son of Joseph Ansell, the founder of Ansell's Brewery. He ran the pub at 133 Cattell Road, the Marquis of Lorne. Although there were no social facilities at the Muntz Street ground, followers would gather at nearby venues, such as the New Inn in Muntz Street, and Sam Gessey's coffee house at the junction of Charles Road and Coventry Road. As well as being a useful footballer, Sam Gessey was also an enterprising businessman, encouraging club players and other Alliance members to use his coffee house facilities, which included billiard tables. This gave his rooms the feel of a gentlemen's club, attracting local residents from all walks of life. The Small Arms Inn was also a popular haunt for the Alliance faithful. On a sizeable corner plot at the junction of Muntz Street and Hawkes Street, with several outbuildings and a large yard, the pub served as a useful gathering place for those connected with the club, which by now had become part of the social fabric of the Small Heath community.

Committee meetings were held a couple of streets away, at the Plume of Feathers pub in Miles Street, an arrangement which had endured since at least the 1877/78 season, and probably earlier. The pub was the favoured choice of the club's senior players who lived close by, and used it as their local. Over time, running the club had become more complex and time consuming, making it difficult for someone in the team to cope with the joint demands of being both club secretary, and player. By 1881/82, the club was entering four cup competitions, itself an administrative nightmare, and the hectic fixture schedule which ensued was just another demanding task for the embattled secretary to sort out. Dates needed to be left free to facilitate each cup draw, and any replays usually led to the urgent rescheduling of fixtures. This was far removed from the more sedate times of the club's early years, when the only pressure was a regular flow of pre-arranged friendly matches, almost always in the local vicinity. How times had changed.

Sometimes the club was able to use ex-players who had recently retired from the first team, such as Philip Harlow in 1881 and Sam Gessey in 1884, but the longer term trend was to turn to their growing group of non-playing members. The club's wider appeal had helped to ensure that it now had a pool of non-playing members ready to put themselves forward for committee work or administrative duties. It was around the summer of 1883 that eighteen year old William Samuel Starling, who worked as a clerk, became the first non-player to be elected as honorary secretary. This break in tradition was born out of necessity, designed to avoid the potential overload from the ever increasing workload. It seems remarkable by modern standards that the club entrusted the job to such a youthful and inexperienced figure, but things were completely different then. The club was being run on an amateur basis and totally reliant on volunteer help from within the ranks of their subscribers. The job of secretary, although prestigious, didn't have any executive powers, except those delegated to the post by the committee, which had grown to sixteen members. The club was run on a completely democratic basis, with the committee voting on any proposals that fell outside the scope of the secretary's delegated powers. In effect, William Starling's job was to ensure that the decisions made by the committee were carried forward, including any paperwork.

The make up of the committee for club's annual meeting in 1884 is quite interesting, being an equal balance of eight players and eight non-players. This ensured that the players retained as much control over club affairs as any other members, and could effectively veto anything they didn't like. The eight players serving on the committee were Ted Bailey, Sam Gessey, Charlie Griffiths, Fred and Tom James, John Jones, Harry Morris and Eddie Stanley. The non-playing members were Alfred Ansell, Albert Coles (secretary of the second XI), Walter William Hart, Philip W. Harlow, C. Holloway, William Starling (secretary), Dr. Thomas and Alfred Jones. Alfred Jones would later make his mark as one of the club's longest serving executives.

After serving out his term, William Starling was succeeded by Sam Gessey, one of the club's greatest servants and still the club's landlord. Having finally called time on his playing career at the end of the 1883/84 season, he remained close to the club by serving as honorary secretary. A popular and well respected figure in football circles, he was an ideal candidate for the job, with a wealth of contacts. His appetite for the job had been stirred by a stint on the local F.A's sub-committee, a position he had been elected to in September 1883.

In the summer of 1885, Walter William Hart, age twenty-six, was elected to the honorary secretary post. A long time member of the Alliance club, he had made a rare first team appearance for them near the end of the 1879/80 season, against Walsall Swifts. In Walter Hart's obituary, written in the *Birmingham Evening Despatch* on 5th June 1940, reference was made to the early club meetings held at the Plume of Feathers, saying "Mr. Hart first became associated with Small Heath Alliance soon after its formation……at a time when meetings were held in a public house in Miles Street." Prior to his involvement, he was already a well known member of the local sporting scene, having played cricket for Small Heath Zingari, with his brother Herbert. He also had the advantage of coming from a well to do, influential family. His father, Matthew Hart, employed over one hundred and fifty staff at his nearby tin plate works, as well as being a respected Alderman on the Town Council representing the Unionist Party. With family connections like this, Walter was used to thinking ambitiously. His natural self confidence, coupled with his innovative style was a breath of fresh air for the club, although his ideas were not universally welcome, particularly amongst the old guard. During his time as honorary secretary, he played a key role in steering the club from amateur to professional status in 1885, and three years later came up with the groundbreaking idea to move the club to "limited company" status. Both ventures were highly controversial at the time, but once Hart had set his mind on the changes, he used all his influence to push them through.

Hart was a leading member of the Birmingham Temperance Society, having first signed the "pledge" at the age of thirteen, and it would be interesting to know what he felt about attending club meetings on licensed premises at the Plume of Feathers. Soon after he became chairman in 1888, the venue was changed to the local Jenkins Street School.

10.2 AN ADVENTUROUS FIXTURE LIST 1883/84

The 1883/84 season was an adventurous time for the Alliance club as it looked to build on the success of it's Walsall Cup triumph. Winning their first trophy had been an important stepping stone, thrusting the club into the limelight both locally and on the national stage. With Will Starling, the first non-player as secretary, the club was able to forge ahead with a busy and enterprising fixture list. Once again the club had entered four cup competitions - the F.A. Cup, the Birmingham Cup, the Walsall Cup, and the Wednesbury Charity Cup - but it was the go-ahead list of friendly fixtures that really show-cased the club's venturesome spirit.

Perhaps the most innovative trip planned was the club's first outing to the London area. A game at Great Marlow, a village on the river Thames between Henley and Windsor, was definitely not the club's usual territory, but demonstrated perfectly their pioneering outlook. My hunch is that the fixture was set up following one of the monthly Football Association meetings in London, where representatives of the two clubs would have rubbed shoulders. Marlow were great supporters of the F.A., and even today are the only club to have appeared in every F.A. Cup competition since it started in 1872. Calthorpe F.C. had been the first club from Birmingham to travel south to London in October 1879, when they were drawn to play at Maidenhead in the F.A Cup first round. However, networking between London and Birmingham clubs for friendly games was rare, with the Alliance leading the way.

In addition, the team was now organising three trips up to Lancashire alone, with games at Accrington, Church, and Great Lever near Bolton. At this time, football in Lancashire was on the rise, attracting numerous players from other areas. The suspicion was that many players were being offered illegal payments to move North. The Great Lever club, for example, had recently enticed several players from the Birmingham district to their ranks. These included Alf Jones, who had joined in the previous season from Walsall Swifts, plus Dennis Hodgetts and Tommy Green for the start of the 1883/84 season. These latter two were described by Great Lever as "two of the fastest and best players from the Birmingham District." Tommy Green frequently flitted from club to club, having already turned out for three prominent Birmingham clubs in the past couple of seasons; St. George's, where he played alongside Hodgetts, Small Heath Alliance, and Aston Unity. Hodgetts also had form in this area. In the previous season, just a week after his regular team, St. George's, had gone out of the Walsall Cup at the semi-final stage against the Alliance, he turned up at the Alliance ground in the colours of Walsall Town.

The season also saw the reestablishment of a fixture with Aston Villa, after a gap of four years. More on that later.

Another intriguing fixture was against the newly formed Dublin Association F.C., Dublin's first association football club. The existence of the fixture would have been lost to history except for a fleeting mention in an article written in 1916, over thirty years after the event. No details are known.

The new season started with some excellent news for the Alliance members. After nearly twelve months on the sidelines, Arthur James was back to fitness and ready for the season's opener at Nottingham Forest's new Lenton ground, the first game ever played there. His recuperation from the severe internal injuries had been painfully slow. After weeks of bed rest and gradual exercise, he now felt fit enough to restart his career. A new rule had been introduced by the F.A. at the start of the season which made a big difference to the style and speed of the game. It was the introduction of the modern two handed throw-in. Previously, throw-ins had been one handed, enabling the ball to be launched over long distances. The ball was often flung straight into the goalmouth at great speed, making the game faster. The new rule brought shorter throw-ins and more passing into the game. Resuming the captaincy, Arthur James came through the game unscathed in the 3-2 defeat.

Incredibly, Arthur's first home game of his come back was against the same fearsome Druids side that had put his career in jeopardy. The Welsh team had been derided by many Alliance followers, who blamed them completely for the long enforced absence of their hero. There is little doubt that Arthur would have been apprehensive about the repeat encounter coming so soon into his return to action, perhaps having flashbacks of the brutal treatment he had received. It wasn't just his physical shape he needed to test out. Did he still have the appetite for the game and the mental resolve to inevitably take further knocks? Unflinching, Arthur bravely lined up in the team, flanked by his two brothers, Tom and Fred. He needed to prove to himself that he still had the mental strength to cope with the physical intimidation that was integral to the Druids' style of play.

The Druids club had sent down their usual combative team to Small Heath. For the past three years they had triumphed in the Welsh Cup, building up a strong team spirit and sense of togetherness in the process, which seemed to make them impervious to any criticisms of their frequent rough play. It was their reputation for an uncompromising style of play, which made them such fearsome opposition. The proud team were both experienced and battle hardened, containing an array of early Welsh internationals.

It was the Druids' defence, renowned for it's strong tackling and physical presence, which ensured that their team's tough reputation still endured. The pairing at the back was burly Robert "Bob" Roberts, said to be a useful boxer, and John "Jack" Powell, a Welsh international who later became captain of Newton Heath. In front of them were the two half-backs; the solidly built Joe Davies, and the smaller, more mobile William Williams. Known as "Little Billy", Williams was feated for his stamina and well-timed tackles, and played in eleven of Wales' first fifteen internationals. Up front, the team was just as robust. John Jones, a coalminer, was given the nickname "Dirty Jack" for his rigorous and, often, over physical approach. The full Druids' team for the game on 29th September 1883 was:

B. Roberts (goalkeeper); J. Powell and R. Roberts (backs); J. Davies and W. Williams (half-backs); J. Jones and J. Doughty (right wing); A. Jones and J. Vaughan (left wing); C. Davies and J. Jones (centres).

John Campbell Orr, one of the Birmingham Association's most respected officials, was asked to referee the match, no doubt in the hope that any residual bad feelings would not be reignited. The build up to the match must have been quite intense, especially for the apprehensive Arthur James. But like all sporting heroes, he was to make a fairy tale return in front of his adoring fans. Within five minutes he had nipped in to score the opening goal. With rain falling incessantly, the "sloppy state of the ground", as it was described in the *Wrexham Advertiser*, made good play more and more difficult. It's easy to imagine players from both sides energetically sliding into tackles, often mistiming them in the slippery conditions. The Alliance clung bravely to their lead until the very last minute, when C. Davies equalised for the Druids, following a free kick. Despite this late disappointment, it had been a good day for the Alliance faithful, watching Arthur James come through the game unscathed and showing signs of his old confidence.

In the Walsall Cup, the first round draw had conjured up a mouth-watering repeat of the previous year's final. Dramatically, the Small Heath Alliance club was again paired with Wednesbury Old Athletic, immediately resurrecting the intense rivalry between the two clubs. It was a cruel way for the Alliance men to start the defence of their trophy. An emotionally charged encounter on hostile territory, with a whiff of revenge in the air, was the last thing they wanted. At the same time, their feelings of trepidation were mixed with a strong determination to keep a tight grip on their trophy, and not fall at the first hurdle. A large contingent of Alliance supporters travelled to Wednesbury to cheer on the cup holders, adding to the spicy atmosphere of the one thousand strong crowd. Both teams were naturally hyped up for the occasion, which turned out to be a bruising and controversial encounter.

It was the Alliance team who scored first, and then have one ruled out for "offside". At half time the score stood at 1-1. In the second half, Old Athletic went ahead, and as they battled to hold on to a 2-1 advantage, one incident in particular seems to have infuriated the Alliance players, when an equalising "goal", just before the end, was ruled out by the referee. The Alliance officials felt so strongly about the unfairness of decision that after the match they immediately lodged an appeal with the Walsall and District F.A. As usual, details of the events on the pitch which led to their appeal are sketchy, but it seems that both umpires had signalled at the same time about separate incidents. The report in the *Athletic News* (7th November 1883) simply stated that the goal was disallowed for "offside", but suggested that it was a legitimate score, and should have been allowed. Whatever the circumstances, the Alliance players obviously felt a strong sense of injustice, and it's easy to imagine the heated exchanges on the pitch. The *Midland Athlete* journal reported that "Partisanship among the spectators was at boiling point and referee, umpires and players were, in turn, consigned to a locality which shall be nameless". In other words, they were ushered away for their own safety.

Later, the committee considering the appeal voted 10-8 in favour of the Alliance, and ordered a replay of the tie to take place. Then farcically the Old Athletic club lodged a counter appeal, and succeeded in getting the decision overturned. This sort of indecision seems typical of many early appeals processes, and it's difficult to know what extra information could have been provided for the committee to be able to reverse their original ruling. Understandably the Alliance club was incensed by the U-turn, but it was still a surprise when, in an apparent fit of pique, the club made the snap decision to resign from the Walsall F.A. The *Athletic News* commented that their stance was justified, and felt that the behaviour of the Walsall Association had opened themselves to ridicule, and doubted "their ability to govern their own affairs". Strong words. The Alliance's retaliatory resignation lasted for two seasons, 1884/85 and 1885/86, as they effectively boycotted the Walsall Cup competition. They had felt genuinely aggrieved by the outcome of the appeal, and as cup holders, they probably felt that their case deserved more consideration. In the end, though, their two year exile from the competition was more damaging to themselves than the Walsall Association, robbing them of vital cup revenue and the chance of further glory. Finally in September 1886 the club applied to be readmitted after again paying an admission fee to the Association.

In their Wednesbury Charity Cup campaign, the Alliance were knocked out in the second round by the eventual runners-up, Nottingham Forest; no further details surviving.

On the last Saturday in November, Great Marlow were the unusual visitors to Muntz Street. "The appearance of a southern team in Birmingham, except in inter-Association contests, is such a rare occurrence now-a-days that the visit of the Great Marlow eleven to Small Heath on Saturday was regarded as quite a phenomenal incident in the history of local football."(*Athletic News*, 28th November 1883). The game ended 2-0 in favour of the Alliance, with Arthur James the best player with his "dodging and tricky dribbling."

10.3 "THE GREAT LOCAL MATCH"

Perhaps the most notable development in the season was the re-emergence of a fixture against Aston Villa, after a gap of four years. It was only the second meeting between the two clubs, hardly an indication of any great rivalry. Since the first encounter in 1879, when the Alliance were victors, Villa had propelled themselves to the top of the local football rankings by winning the Birmingham Cup in three of the last four seasons. It seems that the second encounter materialised after the Alliance veteran Sam Gessey, and Villa captain Archie Hunter, had both been voted onto the sub-committee of the local Association in September 1883. It was surely no coincidence that three months later a fixture had been organised to take place at Perry Barr.

The big talking point was the impressive size of the crowd, with over five thousand people attracted to the game. This was a surprise to most football observers, who hadn't anticipated it. It was on a par with any F.A. cup crowd ever seen at Perry Barr, and way ahead of any Birmingham Cup tie attendance there, which had peaked at two thousand. Part of the answer lay in the vast numbers of Alliance supporters turning up for the occasion. The *Athletic News* (12th December 1883) reported that "the Small Heath inhabitants showed up in strong force, and it was evident from the manifestations of applause when any smart points were executed on either side, that the partisanship was pretty equal."

The Alliance followers had developed an appetite for travelling 'en masse' during the previous season's Walsall Cup triumph. Coincidentally, the tradition had probably all started at Perry Barr, when the ground was chosen as the neutral venue for their semi-final against St. George's. The Alliance fans' relish for a football "day out" was born on that day. It soon became part of their mindset, as large numbers travelled over for their Walsall Cup Final triumph at the Chuckery. The happy memories of that day, and the sense of adventure it created, gave them a hankering to repeat it. They had already travelled in large numbers, earlier in the season, to the Wednesbury Oval for their team's unsuccessful first round defence of the Walsall Cup. Their attention was now focussed on a return trip to Perry Barr, and this time the presence of Aston Villa, the district's top rated club, would add to their determination to make a show. This was just the sort of occasion that the Alliance faithful craved for. To them it was a kind of pilgrimage, and a mass gesture of pride in their home area, Small Heath. Unfortunately for them, it was Villa who came out on top, cantering to an easy 4-0 victory.

It's interesting that during the game's build-up, advertising sheets calling it "The Great Local Match" had been circulating around the streets, whipping up the excitement. It's possible that the Alliance committee were behind some of the advertising 'flyers', producing them to hand out at Muntz Street matches, and circulate around the big local factories, such as the Small Heath gun works (B.S.A.). The fact that three committee men, John and Peter Harlow and Alf 'Inky' Jones, were in the printing trade would have made this a simple operation. It's clear that the population of Small Heath was well primed for the event.

10.4 THE RECRUITMENT OF NEW TALENT

In the meantime, Arthur James' comeback continued to go well until, almost unbelievably, in January 1884 he suffered another serious injury. In a Birmingham Cup replay at the Chuckery Ground, against Walsall Swifts, he unluckily sustained an injury to his neck and spine. The mishap was a complete accident. Mid-way through the second half, the Walsall Swifts' captain, Alf Jones, who had returned from his one season spell at Great Lever, was in possession as Arthur ran towards him to close him down. Just as Jones was hoofing the ball up field, Arthur stumbled and fell forward, receiving the full force of Jones' boot and lower leg on his jaw. Arthur was out cold as the doctor ran on to help him. After play had been held up for fifteen minutes, a still unconscious Arthur was carried to the dressing tent. Fortunately no bones were broken, but his neck was severely strained. On finally regaining consciousness he was taken to a nearby hotel, and later that evening was considered sufficiently recovered to bear being moved to his home.

At first, Arthur's season looked finished. Most people were expecting him to need a prolonged break, but doggedly he managed to be back in action just a fortnight later. He remained hampered by the damage to his neck, and it has been suggested that after the whiplash type injury, he was never quite able to regain his old level of speed and agility. His return to the team, in a friendly against Wolverhampton Wanderers, was marred by severe gales which swept across the country. As a precaution, Sam Gessey had already suggested that the two teams use his coffee house, at the corner of Coventry Road and Charles Road, as a makeshift changing room. Normally competing teams would use canvass dressing tents erected on the edge of the enclosed pitch, but the stormy winds had already made this impractical. By the time kick-off had arrived, the gales in Small Heath had worsened to hurricane force. Resolutely the two teams carried on with the game, trying to play football in the eye of a storm. The winds were so strong that the players could hardly keep the ball on the pitch.

For one player in the Alliance line up, the dramatic proceedings had an extra significance, as he had been invited to play in the game as a trial, by none other than Arthur James. That player was Charlie Simms. By coincidence, he worked at the same factory as Arthur James, the giant Cornwall Works in Soho, also known as Tangye Brothers, and it was here that the Alliance captain had been tipped off about the young worker's football prowess. He was always on the look out for new talent to invite to the club. Over two thousand men earned their living at Tangye's, which specialised in the manufacture of hydraulic lifting machinery. The factory was at the cutting edge of hydraulic technology, providing equipment all over the world. One of their earliest successes, when just a handful of workers were employed, was to assist Brunel with the 1857 launch of the Great Eastern steam ship, after it had got stuck in mud on the edge of the Thames, at Millwall. Using Tangye's specialised hydraulic equipment, the huge ship was successfully manoeuvred into the water. Tangye's famous advertising slogan was, "We launched the Great Eastern, the Great Eastern launched us."

Playing for the Tangye's Works team had been Charlie Simms' first real taste of organised football. The workers would hold regular practice sessions on a vacant patch of waste ground near to the massive factory site and play fixtures with other local teams. At the age of fifteen, early in the 1879/80 season, Charlie was playing for the Works second team, partnering Summers in the half back line against Beech Lanes. Whether this was Larry Summers, who a year later was playing in the Alliance first team, is uncertain, but it's certainly possible that he was another of Arthur James' finds. The Works team was often undermined by having its best players poached, and this eventually led to its reluctant disbandment.

Charlie soon joined another team which played nearby, Handsworth Oakfield. He stayed there for two seasons, 1881/82 and 1882/83, playing alongside another future Alliance defender, Charlie Felton. Both players would be part of the Alliance's 1886 F.A. Cup semi-final team, a fine accomplishment for their old Oakfield club. Charlie's next progression at the beginning of the 1883/84 season, was to join Handsworth Grove F.C., who played at the rear of the local Grove Hotel. It was team captain, Charlie Allen, who had asked him to join and it was during his spell there that senior clubs started to notice him. Aston Villa had been alerted by his performance in keeping their star forward Archie Hunter quiet during a benefit match.

Arthur James knew that he needed to act quickly to head off their interest. His "celebrity" status, as one of the district's top players, was a big pull to aspiring youngsters, but in Charlie Simms' case he also knew his father, William, a foreman blacksmith at Tangye's. As a fender fitter, Arthur was acquainted with most forge workers at the works, and was ideally placed to influence Charlie's father. After all Arthur's groundwork behind the scenes, it was frustrating that Charlie's trial match against Wolverhampton Wanderers should end in disarray, ruined by the hurricane winds. At half time the match was abandoned, by which time most of the two hundred crowd had already scurried away from the field, which was completely open to the elements. Although the storm had taken away Charlie Simms' opportunity to impress, Arthur already knew that he had uncovered a exceptional talent. Charlie was to become one the club's most reliable servants over several decades, both on and off the pitch.

After the curtailed match, the teams dashed back down Charles Road to Sam Gessey's coffee house to get changed, only to find that his front window had been blown into the street by the intense winds. The stormy conditions had also brought an early end to the Alliance's second team fixture at Camp Hill, against the Birmingham Press. It had been an eventful day.

Uniquely, the hurricane force winds had affected football fixtures across the whole country. In Wednesbury, the Birmingham Cup third round tie between Old Athletic and West Bromwich Albion, and the friendly between Wednesbury Town and Aston Unity were both wiped out before half time, and much further north in Blackburn, the representative game between Lancashire and the Birmingham F.As also fell victim in it's early stages. Incidentally, the Birmingham F.A. team featured Archie Vale, the ex-Alliance goalkeeper, who was now with Villa.

Charlie Simms c. early 1884. William Starling, the honorary secretary is peering over his shoulder.

Newcomer Charlie Simms was also a fine cricketer, and each summer after joining the Alliance he teamed up with the local Langley cricket team, for about four seasons. This suggests that, by then, the Small Heath Alliance cricket club had been disbanded. The last mention I can find of it's existence is the summer of 1882.

Another young player increasingly on the Alliance's radar around this time was Harry Morris. A bright and resourceful teenager, his natural territory was along the Coventry Road where he was born. One of six children, he was brought up in a cramped courtyard dwelling at the back of 141 Coventry Road. Leaving Jenkin's Street school at the age of eleven, he was soon bringing money into the family household after finding a job as a tin plate worker in a small workshop. The workshop was known locally as Millington's, after the owner Edwin Millington. Young Harry didn't have far to walk each day, just a short dash across the busy Coventry Road to the workshop at number 152. His father, a one time hackney carriage driver, kept horses. The Coventry Road in the early 1880s was a relentless stream of horse drawn wagons and carriages, bringing people and goods in and out of Birmingham, and it was in this hectic environment that Harry developed his chirpy self-confidence and street savvy charm.

There wasn't much happening on the Coventry Road that the alert and watchful Harry didn't know about, particularly when it came to the football activity taking place at the nearby Alliance ground. During his youth, the Alliance football enclosure was a regular hive of activity with endless kick about sessions and practice games taking place in the evenings, even during the summer period. Then on match days the crowds would flock in to watch their heroes, adding to the general busyness of the area. Enterprisingly, at the age of fourteen he had helped to set up the Small Heath Alexandra club and had soon caught the eye of his more senior sporting neighbours. Nonetheless, Harry was just happy to remain with his pals within the junior ranks, opting to stay with the blue and black horizontal stripes of his Alexandra team.

Arguably, matches in junior football were just as demanding physically as the more senior version, and players like Harry used the games to develop their skills and knack of staying out of harms way. Rough challenges were just as common in junior football as they were in the more illustrious fixtures. One such example came in a 1883/84 junior cup tie between Wednesbury Old Athletic second team and Walsall Rangers. After an Old Athletic player had slipped over, he was viciously kicked as he lay on the ground and needed to be taken off. Assaults like this, it seems, didn't interest referees. During his spell with the Alexandra club, Harry Morris developed into a more than useful outside right and no doubt had often toyed with the idea of joining the Alliance, but he had always remained loyal to his boyhood pals.

During the summer of 1883, though, he started to join in with the evening kick about sessions at the Alliance ground. Harry knew that he wasn't supposed to be there, as he had never paid any "subs", but he still had the brazenness to take part for nothing. Sometimes Eddie Stanley, the Alliance centre forward and committee member, who spent much of his spare time at these evening sessions, would order him out. Then on other occasions he would allow him to stay and play in practice games. After impressing Eddie Stanley he was asked to join, but was still not ready to desert his pals. Soon afterwards he was tempted to take part in a trial game between two selected teams, one labelled "New Cracks" and the other "Old Cracks". The "Old Crocks" team was made up of mainly Alliance first team men, and the "New Cracks" made up of seven youths from Harry's Small Heath Alexandra team, plus four from the Alliance second team. Again Harry made a good impression. Not content with just scoring in the 1-1 draw, he also managed to knock Billy Edden, the "Old Crocks" goalkeeper that day, "through the goal". This touch of daring was typical of Harry Morris. It's interesting that, even though Billy Edden had retired from playing matches, he was still active on the training pitch, as enthusiastic as ever.

Afterwards Harry Morris still played hard to get. The main reason seems to be that his Alexandra team were still engaged in the newly instigated Birmingham Junior Cup competition. The inaugural 1883/84 competition was entered by a mix of second eleven teams from the district's senior clubs, such as Wednesbury Old Athletic, Walsall Town, West Bromwich Albion and Dudley, and teams from ambitious and well organised junior clubs. So alongside the Alexandra club of Harry Morris, there were other junior clubs such as Aston Unicorn, Aston Viaduct, Speedwell, Perry Barr, Fallings Heath Trafalgar and Walsall Rangers. It wasn't until January 1884 that the Alexandra team were knocked out of the new competition, in a second round tie against Walsall Swifts' second team. With one of their half-backs failing to arrive at the Chuckery ground, the Alexandra were forced to play with only ten men and unsurprisingly went down 4-1. The Alexandra team that day was:
Charlie Griffiths (goalkeeper); Charlie Morris (Harry's brother) and Kendrick (backs); Bennett and Hale (half-backs); Pratt and "Skimmer" Page (right forwards); Shaw (centre forward); Jones, captain and Harry Morris (left forwards).

Late in the season Harry Morris finally joined up with the Alliance after they had looked like being a man short for the trip to Accrington. "Butcher" Jones, from the Alliance, had gone to see Harry at his place of work, Millington's, to appeal for his help, and at long last he agreed. In the following season, 1884/85, Harry became a regular in the first team, partnering his hero Arthur James on the right side of the forward line. Over thirty years later, Harry would reveal that when he started his Alliance career, he received payment "in kind". He didn't elaborate, but this suggests that some form of inducement was involved, although not cash.

Future cult hero, Caesar Augustus Llewelyn Jenkyns also first teamed up with the Alliance club during the latter stages of the 1883/84 season. The boss of the Alliance second team, Albert Coles, had been keeping an eye on his progress for a couple of seasons, regularly watching him play on the neighbouring Sunday School pitch. In his previous raids on the Sunday School team, Coles had brought in Alfred Vaughan Jones, a reliable half-back. But in late 1883, the Sunday School team was forced to leave it's home due to the construction of Charles Road. The new road had cut straight through the middle of their pitch, meaning that the adjacent Alliance ground was now enclosed on three sides by roads.

It was just afterwards, that Coles invited the promising Jenkyns to join the Alliance second team. He gave him his first run out on Easter Monday, 14th April 1884, against Aston Morning Star, and he performed so well at centre-half in the 1-1 draw, that just a few days later on 26th April, the seventeen year old novice was drafted into the first team against Wednesbury Town at Muntz Street. It was to be a tough baptism against a top class side, with Jenkyns scoring an own goal in a 4-1 defeat. Yet, despite the difficult afternoon for Jenkyns, Albert Coles had not lost faith in him. He knew that the Welsh born defender had held his own against one of the best teams in the district. Just a couple of weeks later, the same Wednesbury Town team would triumph in the Wednesbury Charity Cup final against a strong Nottingham Forest side. In the following season, Albert Coles nurtured Jenkyns in the Alliance second team, patiently developing his raw talent. He was sure that sturdy defender was worth persevering with, and in the years to follow he was proved right.

As the 1883/84 season drew to a close, it was clear that the club's playing resources had been stretched to the limit. The young talent which had been recruited was much needed during the latter months, as the busy fixture list started to take its toll on the team. The trip to Stoke-on-Trent on 2nd February 1884 proved to be the low point of the season. It was only the club's second visit to the Potteries, following on from last season's 6-1 success at Leek, and it turned out to be a disaster. At kick-off the Alliance team was four men short, and although a further two players turned up after fifteen minutes, the team was trounced 9-1. A week later, for the historic trip to Great Marlow the club only managed to field ten players who battled bravely to limit the score to just a 1-0 reverse.

10.5 PROFESSIONALISM IN THE AIR 1884/85

After the previous season's gradual slump in fortunes, it was clear that the Alliance club was finding it difficult to keep pace with the leading group of clubs. A widening gap was developing, and it wasn't all of the Alliance's own making. The main reason was the proliferation of hidden player payments, now routinely used by unscrupulous clubs to attract players, something the Alliance club tried to steer clear of. Player payments and inducements were completely illegal, but their wide scale use was now giving devious clubs an unfair advantage. One local club at the forefront of this issue, and strong advocates of legalising professionalism in football was Aston Villa.

On 31st October 1884, a Villa club representative travelled to the Dog and Partridge Hotel in Manchester to attend a gathering of thirty seven clubs, intent on forming a new association in direct opposition to the existing English F.A. The group of clubs, almost entirely from Lancashire, had become increasingly frustrated by the F.A's resistance to professionalism, and wanted to force them into a rethink. At the meeting, Villa along with 35 of the other 37 clubs, pledged their support to the new association, and a twelve man committee was elected. Significantly, Villa was the only club from outside Lancashire to make the pledge. Their stance must have sent shockwaves throughout the local Birmingham and District F.A., a strong advocate of amateurism.

Villa's brashness in riding roughshod over their local association's wishes coincided with a huge financial windfall for one of their chief patrons, George Kynoch. In 1884, he had struck a deal for his Lion Works business to be formed into a limited company, an arrangement which netted him a huge amount of cash. With his enormous wealth, and Villa's growing football reputation, they saw the legalisation of player payments and inducements as the obvious way to keep ahead of their rivals; and Kynoch was used to getting his own way. A ruthless businessman, he was prone to unpredictable behaviour. Even his fellow committee men were nervous of his temper, although most of the time he was genial company. The suspicion was that his Lion Works factory was being used to funnel payments to players. It would have been easy for him to list a club player as a "ghost" employee, thus enabling football payments to be hidden as wages. Any illicit dealings would have been almost impossible to trace amongst the company's two thousand strong workforce. It's fair to say that no evidence of any wrong doing has ever been uncovered, but then again, any covert arrangements were never meant to be found out. What we do have however, is clear evidence of Villa's enthusiasm for professionalism, and their naked ambition.

As it happened, Villa's pledge to the new British Football Association soon evaporated. Only 25 clubs actually signed up, with Villa left dithering on the sidelines, not wishing to invite a ban from 1884/85 F.A. Cup competition. However, the cat was out of the bag. It was now clear that Villa could not be trusted to, or indeed was not interested in, towing the party line.

10.6 THREE EPIC ENCOUNTERS AT MUNTZ STREET

On the pitch, it was a frustrating time for the Alliance men, as they struggled to find any kind of consistency. However, amidst the general gloom, three encounters in particular kept the Muntz Street faithful completely enthralled, and tested their emotions to the full. The first two relate to a twice played Birmingham Cup tie against Excelsior, which created unbelievable scenes.

i) The Battle of Muntz Street: Part One, 29th November 1884.

Many football devotees will have heard of the phrases the "Battle of Highbury" and the "Battle of Montevideo", terms given to two particularly violent football encounters from the mid-twentieth century. The violent play during the "Battle of Highbury", the 1934 international between England and Italy, was considered shocking, as were events at the ill-fated 1967 Intercontinental Cup Final replay in Montevideo, Uruguay, between Celtic and the Racing Club from Argentine, when six players were sent-off, and the intervention of riot police was needed to restore order on the pitch. Little known to modern football buffs is a similar story of disarray and violence, which took place at Muntz Street in late 1884, in a twice played Birmingham Cup tie between the Alliance and Excelsior. The two matches were as fierce and unsporting as any recorded during this era.

Initially the rivalry had been on a fairly routine footing, but over a series of cup games, in both the F.A. and the Birmingham Cup, it eventually spiralled out of control, ending in enmity and bitter accusations. The two clubs had first encountered each other in the previous season's F.A. Cup competition. In a hard fought first round match at Muntz Street, the Excelsior club had forced a 1-1 draw to take the Alliance back to their new home at the Aston Lower Grounds. The Excelsior club had only recently moved there after the earlier tenants, the once revered Birmingham Cricket and Football Club, had become defunct. In a tight game, in front of a two thousand crowd, the Alliance went down 3-2 in the replay. Now, a year later, the two clubs were again drawn to meet each other, this time in both the F.A. Cup and the Birmingham Cup.

In the F.A. Cup, the Alliance were again frustrated, losing 2-0 at the Lower Grounds. But it was the next match, in the Birmingham Cup, which really lit the blue touch paper. At the start of the game, the Excelsior team had complained about the "odd" ball that had been put down for kick-off. These protests were brushed aside by the referee, a man who was in for difficult afternoon. Almost immediately from the kick off, Devey (Excelsior) received a severe charge, which left him incapacitated for some time. "The game was of the roughest possible description, and it was nothing but sheer force and rough play that enabled the Heathens" (*Athletic News*) to build up a 2-0 half time lead, with Arthur James scoring the second. In the second half, "they renewed their roughness in a more determined manner than ever, Lovesey receiving an awful kick which compelled him to quit the field.......Bailey, Devey and Barlow were also more or less seriously injured." (*Athletic News*, 3rd December 1884). What's apparent is that referees took little notice of dangerous and rough play, and just left the players to get on with it. In the modern game, it's likely that several players would have been sent off. After around sixty-five minutes of play and the Alliance 2-1 ahead, the game came to an abrupt end when the ball burst. Incredibly, there was no replacement ball available to enable the game to continue, and most people at the ground simply assumed that the Alliance would be given the game.

Afterwards, the Excelsior club made a formal protest to the Birmingham and District F.A. on three different counts. Firstly they protested that the ball, an old one, had been insufficiently inflated and unfit for use. Secondly, they claimed that Arthur

James was off-side for his goal, and finally they complained about the Alliance's violent play. The local F.A. committee ruled that due to the enforced stoppage, the tie should be replayed in its entirety, again at Muntz Street. The Alliance followers were fuming. They had come so close to beating their cup "bogey" team, only for fate to conspire against them. Perhaps in their naivety, they had envisaged that the original 2-1 score line would be allowed to stand, or at most they would be ordered to play out the remaining twenty-five minutes to complete the tie. They were not only frustrated with the local F.A. ruling, but also extremely angry, which put relations between the two clubs under severe strain.

The brutal approach of the Alliance team had left three Excelsior men with severe injuries, with Lovesey, Barlow and Bailey all unfit to play in the replay a month later. Yet ironically, the local F.A. didn't seem to blink an eyelid at the shameful brutal intimidation that had caused their absence.

ii) The Battle of Muntz Street: Part Two, 29th December 1884.

It's quite easy for player animosity to creep into matches when two teams become over familiar with each other, and players become tempted to carry forward feuds from one game to another. That's just human nature. But this tie had now also inflamed the hordes of Small Heath followers, who felt, in their biased eyes, that Excelsior's appeal had been both unsporting, and underhand. Rumours of a "rough reception" that some of them were planning for the visiting Excelsior team were now circulating, and Excelsior soon got wind of this. Would they turn up for the replay? As three and a half thousand spectators assembled for the game, there was no sign of them. Then just a couple of minutes before the kick-off, a covered brake wagon trundled onto the pitch and out stepped the Excelsior team, kitted out and ready for the game. Imagine the drama of the scene, with the hostile crowd initially unsure about what was going on, then realising that it was the visiting players who were climbing out of the wagon. Immediately loud howls of derision then bellowed around the ground.

The thrilling contest which followed ended in a 5-3 defeat for the Alliance. The game itself had passed without incident, but as the Excelsior players were being shepherded back to their brake wagon ready to leave the ground, violence flared up. As the visiting players hurried from the field, a guard of men did their best to fend off the unruly crowd. The guard were members of the Birmingham Boxing Club who had agreed to act as security for the Excelsior contingent. Apparently several Excelsior players were members of the boxing club, and had arranged for their "friends" to help them out. As the players fled, they were pelted with all sorts of missiles. George Jenks, the Excelsior goalkeeper, later recounted that a half brick just missed his head as he made his escape. He claimed that three hundred members of the Birmingham Boxing Club were "on duty" at the match to protect his team. Yet, despite these riotous scenes, the local F.A. didn't feel the need to delve into the issue.

iii) <u>versus Aston Villa - 31st January 1885</u>

This little documented encounter could well lay claim to have been the most exciting Blues versus Villa derby ever. It was only the third time the two clubs had met, both having won one game each, and the occasion served up a breathless seven goal thriller.

At half time the score stood at 2-2. Then after "a lightening run" by Arthur James, he put the Alliance team 3-2 ahead, as the crowd went into overdrive. Could they keep the Villa team, the holders of the Birmingham Cup for the past three seasons, at bay? With three minutes to go, the brave Alliance men were still 3-2 in front. The tense crowd could hardly watch as Villa pushed forward, frantically seeking an equaliser, as the time ticked away. Then it happened. "Out of a scrimmage", Villa forced the ball over the line to make it 3-3. The Muntz Street faithful were distraught. To make matters worse, right on time, Villa scored another scrappy goal, again "out of a scrimmage", to nick the game 4-3.

For the Alliance, it was huge disappointment after coming so close to beating the district's top club. Two months later, Villa won their fourth consecutive Birmingham Cup final.

11
THE START OF THE PROFESSIONAL ERA   1885/86

11.1 HOW THE ALLIANCE COPED WITH PROFESSIONALISM

It was 20th July 1885 when the F.A. members finally voted in favour of legalising professionalism in football. Before this, the balance of power at the F.A. had always been in the hands of the southern amateurs, with support from the Sheffield and Birmingham contingencies, a situation which changed quickly. The threat of a professional breakaway by northern clubs, mainly from Lancashire, but also extending to Aston Villa in Birmingham, finally triggered a new approach by the F.A., who were desperate to retain control under one body. They realised that it was better to allow professionalism under tight controls, rather than cause a damaging split. It was the speed of this tactical change that caught many in the football community by surprise. Almost overnight many old opponents of professionalism were expected to acquiesce with the idea, and allow it to be voted through. Considering the fierce arguments and polarised positions that the issue had generated during the previous couple of years, it's not surprising that many football followers were confused. The clubs themselves were left in a quandary, urgently trying to work out how the new rules would impact on them, and it is often overlooked that some of the biggest repercussions fell on the players who remained amateur. The new F.A rules completely outlawed payments that compensated amateur players for loss of earnings, leaving many worse off. Amateurs could now only claim expenses, such as travel and, if necessary, overnight accommodation. The new rules were practically encouraging them to seek professional status, or be saddled with reduced terms.

Cleverly, the F.A. had also slipped in a couple of new controls as part of the 1885 professionalism deal. These restricted a professional player to just one club a season, and only permitted their involvement in F.A. cup matches if they were born within six miles of their club's ground, or had lived in the vicinity for at least two years. Prior to this, players were free agents and could turn out for who they liked. Now, once a pro-player had signed up for a club at the start of the season, he was ineligible to play for anyone else until the following season.

In Birmingham, where intense opposition to professionalism had thrived, it's clear that many football enthusiasts were finding it hard to come to terms with. Apart from Villa's welcome of the new rules, most local clubs still saw professionalism as an alien concept. The speed of change had caught them unawares. The Small Heath Alliance club was one of those that found itself in a dilemma; it could either stay as an amateur club, and risk an exodus of players, or adopt professionalism. The spectre of professional football caused quite a stir among local football circles, as they struggled to reconcile themselves with the new arrangements. Unlike these onlookers, though, the club didn't have the luxury of time. With the new season only two months away, the Alliance committee had to act quickly. To their credit, with Walter Hart as honorary secretary, they grasped the nettle, and took decisive action to move with the times, and adopt professionalism. Many local football clubs, who stuck to their amateur principles, were soon gone; clubs like Calthorpe, Excelsior, and St George's, all disappeared from the scene during the late 1880s and 1890s.

So how did the Alliance cope with the introduction of professionalism? Secretary Walter Hart worked tirelessly behind the scenes to sort things out for the 85/86 season, and was successful in retaining most of the first team regulars. He soon registered the first team men as professionals, enabling them to be paid a weekly match fee. Player Harry Morris said that, "In the early days (prior to professionalism), the club used to allow me five shillings a match for loss of time, and the money was a God-send to me. When professionalism was legalised we were paid so much a match. This lasted a time and then our club found they couldn't afford it. For a time we were paid according to gate receipts." It was Walter Hart who carried a resolution that the players should be remunerated in this way. From Harry Morris's comments, it seems that the club was in constant danger of slipping into the red, with plenty of uncertainty for the players on how much they would receive.

Some other changes for the players were less obvious. Before professionalism they had been members of a club, paying a weekly subscription. Player payments now meant that their status had subtly shifted from that of a club member to that of an employee, albeit part-time. Obviously this didn't change their relationship with the club overnight, but gradually the club's non-playing hierarchy became more influential. Within three years of professionalism the Small Heath Alliance club was to become a limited company, with a chairman and board of directors completely taking the control of club decisions away from the players.

The second team players were left as amateurs though, largely because the club couldn't afford to include them in the professional deal, and they soon began to make waves. The first team men, protective of their new professional status, were not impressed with their second team colleagues, and the episode soon degenerated into some unseemly internal squabbles. As a result, several second team players left the club.

One of the first to go was prized asset Caesar Jenkyns, who had been carefully nurtured for over a year by Albert Coles, the second eleven coach. He was quickly followed by team mates "Skimmer" Page and Harry Harvey. With loyalty no longer the prime consideration, money more than ever started to influence where players chose to play. Many promising second team youngsters started to have their heads turned by other local clubs who were offering rewards to join them. Unity Gas F.C. cleverly took advantage by enticing several Alliance youngsters to swap clubs. Their new home was just across the Coventry Road, at an enclosure on Green Lane, still in Small Heath. Officially, Unity Gas was an amateur club, but thirty years later, in 1915, Caesar Jenkyns revealed that he had received payment during his two seasons with them.

There were successes, though, with highly rated goalkeeper, Chris Charsley, joining the Alliance. His signing proved that personal contact was still a major factor in influencing a player's choice. During the close season, Alliance new boy Charlie Simms had gone to work in Stafford for a few weeks, where he had come into contact with Charsley during a game of cricket. At this time, Charsley was the regular goalkeeper for Stafford Rangers F.C., but had told Simms that he was moving to Birmingham to join the police force. It was this chance meeting that would enable the club to sign one of the best goalkeepers in the country. He later became the first Small Heath player to gain international recognition with England.

Early in the new year, a few months after the cricket match, Charlie Simms got wind that his pal had started work in Birmingham at Ladywood police station, and along with Alf Jones, the club secretary, the two hurried round to see him. In those days, the police officers "lived-in" at the station, and the enthusiastic Alliance duo got Charsley out of bed to see him. As it happens, the Villa were also trying to sign him, but some indiscreet remarks by one of their players, who said that "Charsley will be about good enough for our second team", had got back to him. Needless to say Charsley soon linked up with the Alliance, and opted to retain his amateur status.

On the surface the impact of professionalism to the Alliance first team players was fairly limited, with no change to their daily lives. They still carried on with their day jobs, with the football payments only acting as a supplementary income to help make ends meet. What's clear is that the Alliance club was unable to compete with the size of payments on offer at richer clubs like Villa. During the 1880s, the Villa club had stolen a march on all of it's local rivals, by totally dominating the Birmingham Cup competition. Between 1880 and 1885, they appeared in six consecutive finals, winning five of them. This not only propelled their popularity within the local sporting fraternity, but also made it easy for them to attract the best players. Success fed their fame, and the money from their successful local cup runs, and prestigious friendlies did the rest.

They were also fortunate to have the patronage of wealthy businessman George Kynoch, who had built his fortune out of the giant ammunitions factory at Witton, known as the Lion Works. He lived like a country gentleman at his Hamstead Hall estate in Handsworth. A keen follower of Villa's fortunes, the Scottish born industrialist frequently watched the games at Perry Barr on horseback, circling the perimeter of the ground as the games took place. On other occasions he would bring his wagon.

Once professionalism had been legalised, the Villa club were able to be more transparent about their inducements to players. A snippet in the *Athletic News* (4th May 1886) revealed that "the latest acquisition to the Villa club is McLeod, the famous Queens Park back, and whose services have been retained at the Lion Works by that enthusiastic sportsman Mr. George Kynoch." William McLeod had played for Queens Park in the 1885 F.A. Cup Final against Blackburn Rovers. Villa's crude inducement for the player was now legal, but it seems almost inconceivable that arrangements like this had not been going on in a covert way prior to professionalism, with the club conniving in the cover up, or at least turning a blind eye.

But even though Villa had finally got their wish to legally pay their players, they still continued to undermine the local association. Like a playground bully, they withdrew from the 1885/86 Birmingham Cup, scratching from their first round tie with Wednesbury Old Athletic, because they felt that, after six consecutive finals, they shouldn't have to play in the earlier rounds of the competition. Villa were now more interested in the national stage, than supporting the local association, and playing one sided matches in the local cup.

However, for all their political posturing with the local association and domination of the local football scene, not everything was rosy at Villa. Behind the scenes, the day to day business of the club was poorly run. A culture of complacency had crept in, with no proper oversight of the club finances. In July 1885 it emerged that the club treasurer had been 'mismanaging' the club finances, leaving it on the verge of insolvency. It was William McGregor who was asked to step in and sort out the mess.

The practice of Small Heath players continuing to work in day jobs alongside their football commitments, continued for several years. In fact the arrangement was positively encouraged by the club. Even seven years later, the club chairman Walter Hart, was still extolling the virtues of having a team of players who worked for a living. At a club dinner, at the Old Royal Hotel in Birmingham in January 1893, he explained why. He put down the success of the club to having "a team of players who not only knew how to take care of themselves, but who followed their daily employment. For a few trifling exceptions, the whole of the Small Heath team worked from Monday morning until Saturday morning." He contended that, "Nothing was more conducive to keep a man in health and make him play football as it should be played, than the following of his employment. To such a man, Saturday came round as a holiday, and he was eager to play. On the other hand, a man who had nothing to do but to loaf about from one week's end to week's end, was not ready for play, and such a mode of life was not conducive to good football."

The first evidence of a Small Heath player actually giving his occupation as a "professional footballer" is contained in the 1901 census records. The player, John Tebbs, was lodging with one of Sam Gessey's brothers, William Gessey, in Wright Street, adjacent to the Muntz Street ground.

11.2 THE ALLIANCE'S STORMING F.A. CUP RUN

During their first season as a professional club, the Alliance stormed through to the semi-finals of the English Cup (the F.A. Cup). Buoyed by a handful of new arrivals, full back James Evetts, and forwards Tom Davenport, Ted Hill and Bill Figures, the team enjoyed the national spotlight with their exploits, becoming the first club in the town to reach the semi-final stage. The excitement generated by the plucky cup run brought a whole new legion of fans to the club. Vitally the luck of the draw gave them the benefit of a home tie throughout the competition. For visiting teams, the Muntz Street ground remained a fearsome place to come.

In round one, Burton Wanderers were the unlucky club drawn to play in Small Heath, suffering a 9-2 annihilation. A heavy downpour persisted throughout the game to the discomfort of the 600 crowd, but the rain didn't put off Eddie Stanley who notched up four goals; the club's first F.A. Cup hat-trick.

Behind the scenes, a sad story was developing. At the age of twenty-nine Arthur James was becoming increasingly frustrated by his inability to regain his old sharpness. His game had always relied on his trickery and speed over the ground, attributes which had been blunted by one injury after another. In despair, he had now decided to call it a day, signing off with a farewell goal against Burton. For seven years he had been the club's most influential player and revered captain. William McGregor wrote in *The Book of Football*, 1906 that "his popularity was similar to that enjoyed by Archie Hunter on the other side of town" at Aston Villa. High praise indeed, considering Hunter's almost legendary status.

His enforced retirement left a huge void in the team, and not least, a new full-time captain was needed. The man asked to step up was John William Hare, who had joined the Alliance at the start of the previous season. Considering that his captaincy coincided with an epic cup run, all the way through to the F.A. Cup semi-final, to this day he remains a total enigma. His exploits have never been given any recognition, in official publications or otherwise, with his contribution to the club's history long forgotten in the passage of time. John Hare was as grafter and not afraid of hard work. He worked as a brass founder, a dangerous and physically demanding job undertaken in remorseless heat. It wasn't for the faint-hearted, standing close to the furnace all day and using brute strength to manoeuvre and pour molten brass. The conditions were merciless, requiring strength of character, physical fitness and a dogged determination. These are all characteristics that he brought to the team. He was a no frills, 'roll your sleeves up' man. This was similar to the team trainer, William Penfield, himself an iron moulder, who could easily relate to the new captain's attributes.

Captain Arthur James stands proudly in front of his players c.1884.

His first game in charge, on 7th November 1885, didn't go well. In an away friendly against a highly rated Derby County side, his team was soundly thumped 6-0. Thankfully the heavy defeat didn't affect the Alliance's cup form. In the second round they overcame the Lancashire team, Darwen, 3-1 at Muntz Street, with two late goals. When Figures scored near the end, after a draw had looked likely, "hats and sticks flew up in the air, and the cheers of the large assemblage was almost deafening."(*Athletic News*, 24th November 1885).

The club now waited eagerly for the third round draw. To their dismay they were paired against the same Derby County team that had given them a football lesson just six weeks earlier. This time the Alliance would be at home, and they knew that they could be a match for anyone on their own patch. Reputations stood for nothing on the rutted and sloping Muntz Street pitch in front of a partisan crowd. The *Derby Daily Telegraph's* report gives a good insight into how the condition of the pitch appeared to psych out the Derby players. It read, "When they (Derby) arrived at the ground it was at once seen that its condition was such as to render good play out of the question and there were anxious shakings of head by the Derby contingent, who seemed to think that the half frozen, half thawed state of the ground made the result far from certain........"

The match was a classic cup tie. In front of 2,000 supporters, the Alliance raced into a 2-0 lead inside the first ten minutes, only to be pegged back to 2-2 just after the hour. Then, with only fifteen minutes left, they sent the crowd wild as they edged 3-2 in front. For good measure they added a fourth right on ninety minutes to win 4-2. The result was a big upset in the football world, and a great credit to captain "Jack" Hare and his brave team. The *Derby Daily Telegraph* report continued, "The visitors (Derby) were all abroad on the treacherous turf, and the miss kicks by the backs were as numerous as the mistakes made by the forwards. On the other hand, the home team, who were much lighter, played up splendidly and they fairly revelled in the horrible state of the ground."

There is no doubt that the speed and lightness of foot over the muddy surface were great assets for the Alliance players. In the earlier 6-0 friendly defeat at Derby, the *Derby Mercury* had commented on "the Brum's.....fast team, with a very smart right wing." The smart right wing was Tommy Davenport, playing in Arthur James' old position. Even thirty-seven years later, in January 1923, the Derby Daily Telegraph was still writing about the state of the pitch, and how the water from a partial thaw had hidden dangerous ice, which had remained below the water in the furrows. Apparently at half time, the Derby team, backed by their travelling committee members had made a vociferous protest to the referee, Mr. W. H. Jope from Wednesbury, but to no avail. They were told that any complaint should have been lodged before the match had started.

After receiving a fourth round bye, the Alliance were drawn at home to Davenham in the fifth round, a small town between Crewe and Runcorn, just south of Northwich in Cheshire. On a fine afternoon an impressive crowd of 6,000 packed into Muntz Street. Small Heath was now in the grip of cup fever, with the attendance ten times bigger than the first round tie against Burton Wanderers. Having won the toss, the Alliance chose to defend the Muntz Street goal, sometimes called the entrance end. Presumably they were keen to attack towards Muntz Street in the second half, where their most partisan fans were situated. It was a fast and exciting match, shaded 2-1 by the Alliance.

For the sixth round, the quarter finals, Redcar from Teeside made the long trip south. The usual custom was to send someone down to the railway station to officially welcome visiting opponents. Craftily, the Alliance also usually sent a second person to secretly gather information on the strengths of their opponents and their key players. For the arrival of the Redcar team, Charlie Simms did the detective work, finding out that they possessed a "flyer" at outside left. As the Alliance right back, this was of particular interest to him, as he prepared to do a tight marking job on his speedy opposite number. In these days, man to man marking was called doing a "policeman". The Redcar team and officials were shown to the Grand Hotel in Birmingham, described in the press as "a noted football house". It's likely that the players packed into two or three rooms to keep the costs down.

The press in the north-east (*The North Eastern Daily Gazette*, 9th February 1886) had been sure that Arthur James would be in the Alliance team, pronouncing with a hint of sarcasm, that he would "re-don his jersey for positively another last time." Their assumption was based on an ongoing injury saga to one of the Alliance's right sided forwards (thought to be Harry Morris). In the previous round, against Davenham, he had suffered a seemingly innocuous graze to his shin, which eventually turned septic. The speculation was that the dye in his sock had caused blood poisoning, a potentially dangerous condition. Bravely, he was patched up for the sixth round, even though he wasn't fully fit, and Arthur's speculated call-up didn't happen. In front of another bumper crowd of around 7,000 excited spectators, the Redcar team was brushed aside 2-0, with Tommy Davenport scoring both goals. Especially for the tie, the club had erected some temporary grandstands procured from the Birmingham and District F.A., which were filled to capacity. It was the first time that the ground had been able to offer seating facilities for spectators, although the vast majority of the crowd still packed the standing areas.

The victory set up an intriguing semi-final against a strong West Bromwich Albion team at Aston Lower Grounds. By now, new goalkeeper Chris Charsley had joined the Alliance, but he wasn't eligible to play in the semi-final, even though he had played in a couple of friendly fixtures immediately prior to the big match. The F.A. rules stipulated that a player must be registered with a club for at least a month to be eligible for cup matches. This was good news for the incumbent Tom Hedges, who had played in all the previous rounds.

The day of the semi-final, 6th March 1886, was a proud one for Fred James. The club he had helped to set up was playing in its first F.A. Cup semi-final, and he was the sole surviving member of the club's first football fixture in 1875. Back then Fred James was the youngest player in the team, just turned seventeen, but now he was the most experienced and longest serving player, playing in his final season before retirement. It was the biggest match in the club's history and Fred James was no doubt hoping that after one more win, he could end his career at the Kennington Oval in the F.A. Cup Final. But first local rivals West Bromwich Albion were standing in the way of his dream.

Fred James

Due to the fame of the F.A. Cup competition, and the national interest in the match, the rivalry and excitement amongst the local partisans was naturally high, and intensifying as the match got closer. There had never been a more eagerly awaited game staged in Birmingham. It was a pity, therefore, that the bitterly cold weather, and the two to four inches of frozen snow covering the pitch, made it a difficult day for spectators and players alike. Yet despite the freezing weather, and slippery conditions underfoot, crowds doggedly flocked to ground, determined to enjoy the occasion and cheer on their team. The following eye witness account from the *Athletic News* (9th March 1886) describes the build up:

"Long before the hour appointed for hostilities, there was a constant procession of charabancs, omnibuses, waggonettes, brakes, drays, cabs, cars, and vehicles (all horse drawn) of every conceivable description, whilst foot passengers bustled onwards in their thousands, evidently anxious to be in time to secure a good view of the proceedings. On arriving at the ground shortly after three o'clock, the scene which met my gaze was of an extraordinary character, and at a rough estimate there must have been something like 12,000 spectators present. The pavilion and grandstands were packed to excess, vehicles, which formed a double row right round the outer part of the circuit, being crammed with occupants, whilst the roofs of all the pavilions, refreshment bars, and the house tops in the immediate vicinity were crowded. Trees were swarmed, and in fact, every conceivable coign of advantage was occupied by the anxious throng of sightseers."

At 3.10 p.m. the teams ran out to loud cheers, Small Heath Alliance kitted out in a newly unveiled strip of chocolate and white halved shirts. Many supporters in the raucous crowd wore "pasteboard" on their hats denoting their club allegiance, which displayed either "Play Up, Alliance", or "Play Up, Albion". These were sold in the streets outside the ground, and are probably among the earliest examples of football souvenirs. The Albion version included a picture of a throstle sat on a cross bar. There was plenty of banter and ridicule caused by these new adornments, as opposing fans easily identified each other.

The match was a disaster for the Small Heath men. 2-0 down at half time, they never managed to get a foothold in the game, eventually losing 4-0. The *Athletic News* (9th March 1886) described the scenes which occurred during the closing minutes of the game. "Party feel ran uncommonly high, and occasionally an outburst of temper was displayed which promised to culminate in a row, and sure enough, towards the finish, a general melee ensued, which commenced on the dressing tent side, where the majority of the betting fraternity usually assemble. The outbreak took place about five minutes before the termination of the match by a gang of the great unwashed element commencing to snowball a contingent of Black Country people who occupied one of the vehicles, and in a very short time a complete bombardment was going on, which resulted in the crowd breaking onto the field of play, and there hostilities were carried on with renewed vigour. Bob Roberts (the Albion goalkeeper) was the recipient of a shower of snowballs, and had to skedaddle off at top speed, and he, in company with the whole of the Albion players, came in for a full share of frozen snow before they could reach the dressing tent. It was a most disgraceful occurrence, and casts another stigma upon the Brummagem roughs, which it will take a long time to eradicate."

As stewards and police fought to restore order, the unruly mob dashed towards the exits hurling bricks, tin cans, buckets, chairs and lumps of ice, an indication of the freezing cold conditions, at anyone who got in their way. One serrated can struck an unlucky carriage driver who lost an ear. The crushing defeat was a major disappointment for Small Heath and in particular the 27 year old Fred James. His hopes of making his last Alliance appearance in the F.A. Cup Final had been swept away in dramatic fashion. It was a cruel way to end his career. Later, each player would receive a payment of half a crown (twelve and a half pence) for playing in the match, plus one shilling and sixpence (seven and a half pence) for a meal and a shilling (five pence) for the cab fare (horse drawn) to and from the ground. As Fred made his way home in the two mile cab ride, his thoughts might have flashed back over his career and to his pioneering team mates from the first ever match in November 1875 and how it had all started.

The semi-final appearance had given the Alliance club national coverage. In the strong footballing area of Sheffield, the view on Small Heath's achievement was mixed. An article in the *Sheffield Independent*, on the Tuesday following the game, offered only half hearted praise saying:

"Small Heath Alliance have come well forward during the present season, and are to be highly complimented on the bold front they have shown, but still they have been somewhat fortunate in the draws, not having met, up to Saturday, any first class teams, though they have defeated some very fair average clubs. In the Birmingham district they are not reckoned as one of the leading combinations by any means, and, given a fair day and a fair field, I could enumerate several that, on public form, are able to give them the go-by."

The term "given a fair field" is quite interesting, giving the impression that the Alliance's Muntz Street ground was unfair to visiting teams. The unfavourable state of the pitch had obviously reached the notice of the Sheffield sporting press. Given that the Alliance were drawn at home in each round, the inference is that the pitch was at least partly responsible for their excellent progress. The article continued:

"The fact remains, however, that they have worked their way into the semi-final of the great competition, and no doubt feel proud of the position. The Albion men, on the contrary, have been able to hold their own against the strongest teams that could be brought against them, and have nearly an unbroken record for the season. Birmingham spectators are not the most pleasant to play before, particularly if their favourites are playing a losing game, as on Saturday. It appears a few minutes before time was called, the crowd broke onto the field of play, and it was impossible to play quite full time, which is much to be regretted, as these exhibitions only tend to bring the town into disrepute and cannot in any way assist the club on whose behalf the disturbance is created. Instead of the crowd being pleased at good play - as they should be, no matter by which side shown - they pelted Roberts, the Albion goalkeeper (perhaps the best in England) with snowballs, as well as several of his confreres."

The scenes of disturbances in the crowd caused consternation within the local football authorities, so much so that the president of the Birmingham F.A., Charles Crump, who had witnessed the ugly scenes, arranged for extra police from Birmingham to be drafted in for the Cup Final. This seems to be the first recorded occasion of any football authority accepting some responsibility for the behaviour of the crowd by paying for additional policing. *The Yorkshire Post* (12/3/1886) reported:

"In consequence of the disgraceful behaviour of some of the crowd in snowballing at the football match at Birmingham last Saturday between West Bromwich Albion and Small Heath Alliance for the English Cup, the Birmingham F.A. has decided to employ a force of police for the cup final tie tomorrow (3rd April) to apprehend all rowdies interfering with players, and will pay the expense of a prosecution before the magistrates."

Sadly, J. H. Cofield, the honorary secretary of the Birmingham and District F.A. since 1880, and responsible for organising the semi-final, had passed away before the cup final. His co-ordination of the Lower Grounds event had been his last official act. With his health in terminal decline, he had bravely put all his effort into organising it, before succombing just three weeks later.

11.3 RIVALRY WITH ASTON VILLA IGNITED

The Alliance's epic F.A. Cup run really got under the skin of the town's most esteemed club, Aston Villa. It wasn't that the Small Heath men had overtaken them as a football force, as it was clear that the Villa club still held the ascendancy. No, what peeved them was the Alliance's new found celebrity status and national glare of publicity. Sure, the Villa held the upper hand, but it was the Small Heath team who were now the focus of attention in the town, and Villa didn't like sharing it. Unknown to most of the crowd, the whole Villa team attended the big match, gazing out enviously from the Lower Grounds pavilion. They weren't due to be there, but by coincidence their scheduled game at Derby County had been called off due to the freezing conditions. It gave them an unexpected opportunity to witness the greatly anticipated event, which, at the time, was the town's biggest ever football occasion. Despite Villa's complete dominance in local competitions, they had never reached this stage of the F.A. Cup, and were no doubt seething that another Birmingham club, the Alliance, had stolen the spotlight.

Before this episode, the two clubs had never considered themselves to be fierce rivals, only ever meeting on three previous occasions, none of them competitive. The Alliance had developed a far greater rivalry with at least three other clubs, all fired by memorable cup battles; Wednesbury Old Athletic (9 competitive meetings), Excelsior (5 competitive meetings) and Aston Unity (4 competitive meetings). Their cup exploits and growing status, however, had put them in Villa's firing line. The watching Villa players were keen to reassert themselves as undisputed top dogs in the town, and quickly arranged a home and away contest with their new antagonists. Three weeks later, the Villa team visited Muntz Street determined to quell their rival's advancement up the pecking order. The rivalry had well and truly been ignited. The Alliance dared to take an early lead, Harry Morris scoring, but by half-time were 4-1 down. Villa added four more in the second half to humiliate the Alliance 8-1. Two months later, the Small Heath men went to Perry Barr only to suffer another crushing defeat; this time 7-0, in what would be Fred James' final game before retiring. In the Villa team was their new professional from Queens Park (Glasgow), William McLeod.

Despite the Alliance being a long way behind the town's top club in terms of playing strength, they had managed to provoke a mutual rivalry. Villa had been drawn in, and the two sets of partisan supporters did the rest. The following season, 1886/87, home and away fixtures were again scheduled, this time in unusual Monday afternoon timeslots. The matches were now assuming an importance way above any rational logic, labelled in some quarters as the "championship of Birmingham"(*The Athletic News*, 2nd November 1886). The two teams battled out a 1-1 draw at Muntz Street, where the fervour generated can be appreciated from this extract from the match report in the *Athletic News*:

"I do not wish to detract an iota of credit which is justly due to the Heathens for the plucky fight they made, because they stuck manfully to their task right to the conclusion of the game and responded to the calls of their excited partisans to "Play up" or "Stick to it" in a most persistent and praiseworthy manner; but, at the same time, it is foolish for some of the hot headed Small Heath patriots to allow their feelings to run away with their judgement in the manner they do."

The return match at Perry Barr in January 1887 turned out to be a real thriller. The Alliance were 2-0 up with only ten minutes remaining, yet somehow contrived to concede three late goals and lose 3-2.

Throughout the season, Villa's primary target had been to get to the F.A. Cup final, and consign the Alliance's semi-final appearance to history. By February they had achieved their goal, and revelled in the opportunity to book a third fixture with the obliging Alliance men just four days before the Final. The timing was clearly designed to torment the Alliance club and give Villa supporters an opportunity to gloat. Dramatically, the match day at Perry Barr coincided with the visit of Queen Victoria to Small Heath; Wednesday 23rd March 1887. The Queen's visit meant that there were an estimated half a million people lining the streets from Small Heath station, where she was arriving, to Birmingham Town Hall. *The Times* newspaper (24th March 1887) seemed eager to point out, rather ungraciously, that "at least two thirds of this number belonged to what are probably the roughest classes of the population of England."

Two hours before the Royal train's one o'clock arrival, all traffic was stopped from entering the Coventry Road procession route, and the streets lined with police and various volunteer regiments. The Queen's schedule included a carriage ride around Small Heath Park, before parading down the Coventry Road and Bordesley High Street, into the town centre. It was through all of this hustle and bustle, and the thronging crowds that the Alliance players would have made their way to the Villa ground for their afternoon kick off. The game resulted in a resounding 7-0 victory for Villa as they warmed up for the Cup Final. Apart from the score line, the game was ignored by the press, as all the focus was on the Royal visit.

The following day, the Villa players and officials travelled to Holt Fleet, a small village in the Malvern Hills on the river Severn, to prepare for their big day. On the Saturday, Villa beat West Bromwich Albion 2-0 to lift the cup, the first time it had come to Birmingham. Trying to keep up with Villa was soon outside the means of the Small Heath club, as Villa's wage bill grew to seven times greater than the Alliance's by 1888. With differences like this, it was always going to be an uphill struggle for the Alliance.

12
ON THE FINANCIAL TREADMILL 1886/88

12.1 ALF "INKY" JONES ELECTED HONORARY SECRETARY

Alf Jones took over the reins as club secretary from Walter Hart in the summer of 1886, ready for the club's second year of professionalism, at a time when the new rules were starting to bite. The timing of his tenure meant that he was thrown right in at the deep end. Yet when he first arrived in Small Heath in 1882, he was a most unlikely candidate to become involved with a football club. Previously in his native Shropshire, he hadn't shown the remotest interest in football and had no football playing credentials whatsoever. His lack of athleticism and diminutive frame meant that he had never considered playing the game. The son of a Wellington publican, he had concentrated all his efforts on successfully completing his printing apprenticeship, which eventually led to him taking a printing job in Small Heath as a compositor.

So how did his conversion to football take place? Like all these things, fate played a large part. On moving to Small Heath, by chance Alf had rented a house in Muntz Street, right in the heart of Alliance territory, but it was only after an off the cuff suggestion from his wife Sarah (nee Powis), to watch one of her relatives play for Saltley College, that his interest was first stirred. Saltley College was a nearby teacher training establishment, whose ready supply of students made them a useful team during the late 1870s and early 1880s. Two brothers from the Black Country arm of her family, Samuel and John Powis, were past students and now both worked as school masters in Wednesbury and Rushall respectively. Students would turn out for Saltley College during their two or three year course, and often join up with their home town club afterwards. Samuel Powis became a regular member of the Wednesbury Strollers' team between 1879 and 1883, including an F.A. Cup tie against Aston Villa. During this period though, he still went back to Saltley College each year for the annual re-union event, when a football match would be played between the "Past" and "Present" students on the college grounds. It is likely that it was the re-union match in 1882 that Sarah and Alf Jones attended to watch him play.

A week later, Alf Jones went along to see the Alliance against Walsall White Star. Although the White Star team never turned up, it had been his first visit to the Muntz Street ground and his first contact with the Alliance club. With his new found interest, he was soon a regular face at matches, developing a strong attachment to the club. By another twist of fate, Alf's job as a printer's compositor was in the same line of work as two prominent committee men, brothers John and Philip Harlow. In fact, Philip

Harlow, a fellow printer's compositor, was club secretary in 1882, and this may have been just the encouragement Alf needed to get involved. Just a couple of years later in 1884, Alf was voted onto the committee for the first time. He once joked that the only reason he was able to gain enough votes, was because several members thought that they were voting for one of the players, also called Alf Jones (Alfred Vaughan Jones), but this was typical of his self-deprecatory style. With his hands always seemingly covered in ink from his printing work, he soon acquired the nickname of "Inky" Jones.

12.2 CHALLENGING TIMES 1886/87

As the new season approached, the Alliance club was at a crossroads, eager to build on the success of it's cup exploits. Would the club be able to push it's way into the top tier, or would it be held back by lack of funds? The windfall from the cup run had been a welcome bonus, but any spending needed to be sustainable. To many observers, the Alliance had already been punching above their weight, yet the expectations of their fervent supporters had now gone into orbit. Fortunately, the new honorary secretary, Alf Jones, was a man with a cool head and not one to get carried away with all the hype. He quietly went about his job, seeking out fresh blood to add to the club's experienced core of players.

With the retirement of Fred James it seemed like the end of an era. He was the last player with direct links to the club's embryonic days of 1875 on the Arthur Street wasteland. Throughout Fred's eleven year career, loyalty and commitment had been uppermost in the team's ethos, coupled with an inbuilt pride of representing their own neighbourhood. Now things were changing. The advent of professionalism had challenged this concept of loyalty, replacing it with a more mercenary attitude and creating a market place for players. Alf Jones didn't have an easy job. He only had limited funds to work with, yet the club followers had sky high expectations. The vociferous nature and unquestioned allegiance of the Small Heath supporters was a well known feature of the club, a phenomenon that mystified many press observers. They couldn't understand how a club with only a single trophy success, the Walsall Cup in 1883, could command such loyalty. They could easily explain the enthusiasm of the Villa support, as they had been fed on success after success in the Birmingham Cup, with five wins since 1880. Yet the partisanship of the Small Heath followers hadn't been driven by trophy success, it was purely out of loyalty for the club. The *Athletic News* (16th March 1886) commented that the teams of both the Alliance and Aston Villa were "looked upon as idols far above this worldly sphere" by their supporters. The in-built loyalty of the Small Heath folk was a great asset, but it also put great pressure on the club committee to make swift progress.

Generally, it was a torrid time for club administrators like Alf Jones, as they struggled to come to terms with the rigid new rules introduced a year earlier to police professionalism. It was also a tough time for local associations as clubs tested them out with appeals. One of the most common appeals came from professional players wanting to be restored to the amateur ranks, in order to change clubs. As a "pro", a player was limited to one club per season, so if he lost his place, it was only natural for him to try and avoid this stipulation by cancelling his professional registration mid-season. Just two months into the season, the Crosswell Brewery club had put in a request to the Birmingham and District F.A. for six players to revert back to amateur status, but like most other requests, it was politely declined in order to maintain some semblance of order and discourage abuse of the system. Sometimes, clubs and players simply ignored the rules, but this led to an increase in disciplinary hearings called to deal with any suspected violations. Several clubs, including Villa, St. George's, and Wednesbury Old Athletic were summoned to the local association to explain themselves on this issue.

There's little doubt that the impact of professionalism, now in its second season, was starting to bite. Quickly, the gap between the more prosperous teams and the rest began to widen, as financial clout became a key ingredient of success. For many aspiring clubs like the Alliance, it suddenly became more difficult to keep pace with the top ranked clubs. Yes, they were a professional club, but their inability to compete financially for the best players meant that they were slipping down the pecking order. It was a vicious circle prompted by their lack of trophy success. It is against this backdrop that Alf Jones worked to strengthen the team. His most pressing job was to find a replacement for Fred James; not an easy task. With many potential second team successors, like Caesar Jenkyns, already enticed away, Alf Jones was forced to look outside the club for his man. His approach was to trawl rival clubs within the town for players open to a move, or take on quality cast offs who had been prematurely discarded. One such player was George Price from Aston Villa, who was perhaps Alf's shrewdest acquisition. Originally a St. George's player, his vast experience had included St. George's historic match against Preston North End, on their first ever appearance in Birmingham on 11th October 1884. Two weeks after this landmark match, he joined Villa, becoming a regular member of Villa's half back line for two seasons, a stint which culminated with a winners medal in the 1886 Birmingham Charity Cup final. Now, with his place at Villa no longer secure, he made the switch to the Alliance. He was a player with an undoubted football pedigree and was seen as a fitting replacement for Fred James.

Also joining the Alliance for the new season, were the Excelsior duo Freddy Barlow, a half-back and Jim Lovesey, a defender. The pair had been team mates at Excelsior since 1883, apart from Lovesey's short spell at Villa between February and May 1885. New players were no longer free, all expecting appearance money and adding to the club's outgoings. The club didn't go overboard, but coping with the unrelenting strain of weekly player payments became an all consuming chore, robbing the club of its previous carefree spirit. Alf Jones' immediate answer to grappling with the new financial obligations was to arrange for most of the club fixtures to be played at home, ensuring that he had a regular stream of much needed gate money. Incredibly, around 80% of the 1886/87 fixtures were played at Muntz Street. Moreover, of the thirty home games played, only one opponent was from outside the confines of the Midlands; an early season visit from Halliwell in Lancashire. Had Jones calculated that he would get better gates against more local teams? Vitally his plan kept the club solvent, but there was a downside. The Alliance was fast becoming an inward looking club, shrinking its horizons and sphere of influence. Any national recognition it had gained during the previous season's cup run was quickly evaporating. Only eight away trips were undertaken all season, presumably to cut costs, the furthest journey being to Stoke. They did have one fresh venture, accepting an invitation to take part in the Derbyshire County Charity Cup, an eight team competition promoted by the Derby Association.

On the field, the season turned out to be a scrappy one, littered with erratic performances, including eight defeats at home. Perhaps the most devastating setback was the club's early exit from the F.A. Cup, knocked out at the first hurdle, and immediately taking away the chance of another exciting cup campaign. A five thousand strong crowd had packed into Muntz Street, only to see their heroes outgunned 3-1 by a resurgent Mitchell's St. George's team, a newly formed alliance between the renown St. George's club and Mitchell's Brewery. Shrewdly, St. George's had negotiated a fruitful sponsorship deal with the local brewery to bring in much needed funds to boost the team. It was an innovative approach to coping with the added financial pressures brought on by professionalism.

An interesting snippet in the *Athletic News* (5th October 1886), within the regular 'Derbyshire Jottings' column, mentioned that Derby St. Luke's had played that week "on the *coffee ground* at Small Heath." This is the only time I've come across this unusual description of Muntz Street, and I'm wondering what prompted it. Two suggestions come to mind. Could it be an oblique reference to Sam Gessey's coffee house next to the ground, on the corner of Coventry Road and Charles Road, which could easily have been the regular haunt for post-match socials with the visiting team? If so, it could be a signal that teetotaller, Walter Hart, was now exerting his influence on this matter. A more off the wall suggestion is that used coffee beans and dregs from the coffee house were used to level off the ruts and furrows on the pitch, perhaps giving it an aroma of coffee.

Come November, the Alliance's sporadic form saw them crash out of the Walsall Cup 3-0 at the hands of West Bromwich Albion, who had only sent over a team of reserves. Quite clearly the team was going backwards, ominously described in the *Athletic News* (27th November 1886) as "going down the nick" and "on the slide". Even amongst this turmoil, though, the team still had the capacity to surprise, and doggedly embarked on a fine run in the Birmingham Cup. The campaign began with a resounding 7-0 victory against Stafford Road, then after a bye in round two, the team cruised past Coseley 13-0, in a tie that goalkeeper Chris Charsley never handled the ball once during the entire game; surely a unique record.

In the fourth round tie against Derby Junction, plenty of drama was generated even before the ball was kicked, with both teams protesting to the referee (W.B. Mason of Aston Villa) about the dangerous state of the Muntz Street pitch. Days of sub-zero temperatures had left the playing surface rock hard, with razor sharp mud ridges caused by the deep frost. With indecisiveness from the referee, both teams courageously went ahead with the tie, which saw the Alliance complete an easy 4-0 win. However, due to the pre-match protest, the result was subject to a special hearing by the Birmingham and District F.A. at the Grand Hotel on the following Wednesday,

Protesting to the local F.A., on all kinds of issues, was an accepted part of the game during this era. Every local F.A seemed to be bogged down by the incessant stream of protests submitted by peeved club secretaries, as they attempted, as a last resort, to get a result overturned. The Derby Junction club seemed to be serial protesters. Earlier in the month, they had lodged one with the Derbyshire F.A., after they had been knocked out of the Derbyshire Cup by Heeley, a Sheffield club. Not content with protesting about one issue, they had listed four for good measure. These were:
1. Heeley won by rough play (later withdrawn).
2. Heeley's ground was not in a proper condition to play.
3. It was a neutral ground, and their consent to play there had not been obtained.
4. The ground was located in Yorkshire, half a mile outside Derbyshire.

Like most protests of this nature, they were thrown out because the objections about the pitch and it's location had only been made after the match. However, the protest about the state of the Muntz Street pitch had been made before the Birmingham Cup tie had kicked off, and had even been supported by the home team, leaving the Birmingham and District F.A. with no choice but to order a rematch. Just three days after the appeal, the fourth round tie was replayed, and again the Alliance were victorious, progressing 1-0 into their first Birmingham Cup semi-final. The win gave the club a huge lift, and soon afterwards there was more good news, when it was announced that their old hero, Arthur James, was set to make a surprise return to the team. His unexpected comeback began with the home friendly against Burton Wanderers on 5th February 1887, immediately stirring memories of his former pomp. Like all true greats, he played as if he had never been away, even scoring a goal in the 2-0 win. His fine performance led the *Athletic News* to comment that he "displayed a lot of his old skill and cleverness, indeed his exhibition is said to have been brilliant, and I hope he will now be seen more frequently on the field, as he was always a popular footballer."

Arthur James had been away from the game for fifteen months, with no hint of a return, so what was going on? It seems likely that the whole idea had been contrived to help deflect the growing unease concerning the lack of progress being made at the club. There's no doubt that Arthur's reappearance injected some much needed cheer into the club, but was he fit enough for a sustained comeback? Now aged thirty, and hampered by his poor level of fitness, it was never likely to be a long-running affair, but his presence seemed to have an uplifting affect on his team mates. Throughout February, the team remained unbeaten, with three wins and a draw, spurred on by Arthur's poise and experience. Then came the big match at Aston Lower Grounds; the Birmingham Cup semi-final against Long Eaton Rangers.

Rangers had first entered the Birmingham Cup in 1883, following in the footsteps of several other Derbyshire clubs; Derby (not County) 1879, Spital 1880, Burton Strollers, Derby Midland and Derby St. Lukes 1881, and Ashbourne 1882. Until now, Rangers had failed to make an impact, but this season they had built a strong reputation as resilient cup fighters. Earlier, in three rounds of the Derbyshire Cup, they had scored thirty-eight goals without reply (Sawley Rangers 17-0, New Whittington Rovers 17-0, and Matlock 4-0), and in total had lost only one of eleven cup ties played so far this season. Their team had strength in depth, backed up by an impressive pool of nearly sixty playing members, including several from the Derbyshire Association representative team; goalkeeper F. Start, half-back B. Stevenson, and left wing pairing Hardy and Vessey. Moreover, they had already beaten the Alliance 4-2 on an early season visit to Muntz Street. It's not surprising, therefore, that they arrived at the Aston Lower Grounds full of confidence. The form of the Alliance had been more sketchy, although over the past few weeks the team had maintained a good level of consistency, thanks to the steadying influence of Arthur James. Nevertheless, they knew they were in for a tough afternoon.

As both teams ran out the weather was atrocious. Thick snow was falling, and being driven across the pitch by a strong wind. The near blizzard conditions had understandably kept the crowds away, with only 650 diehards braving the elements. If the occasion had been ruined for spectators, it was just as bad for the players. When play started it was almost impossible to see the ball in the blinding squalls. Unperturbed, the Alliance team started to take control, with goals from Harry Morris and Eddie Stanley, as they battled to a 2-0 half-time lead. It was a lead that didn't last. As the snow eased off in the second half, Long Eaton Rangers clawed their way back with two goals, living up to their 'never say die' reputation. The Alliance had let their chance slip, and the game turned out to be Arthur James' final appearance. His comeback trail had lasted only five games, his body no longer able to endure the physical demands of weekly games.

In the replay, a subdued Alliance, minus Arthur James, stumbled to disappointing 2-0 defeat, wasting a golden opportunity to appear in their first Birmingham Cup Final. It was no consolation that Long Eaton Rangers went on to lift the trophy, surprising everyone by beating the red-hot favourites, West Bromwich Albion.

Harry Morris

In the final month of the season, the Alliance took part in the Derby County Charity Cup competition, an indication that the club was, perhaps, short of options in finding fixtures. Charity contests had quickly become less appealing to many higher ranking professional clubs, who now often shunned them in order to play more lucrative games elsewhere. Only last season, the same competition had attracted three clubs destined to be founding members of the Football League (Aston Villa, Bolton Wanderers and Notts County), but their priorities had changed almost overnight. To them, charity competitions were a throwback to the out-and-out amateur days, when raising funds for good causes was still a prevailing consideration, a sentiment which had been rapidly overtaken by the need to increase income for player wages. Aston Villa, for example, caused ripples by scratching from the final of the 1887 Birmingham Charity Cup against Wolverhampton Wanderers.

The Derby County Charity Cup was a kind of hybrid competition. In the first round clubs were allowed to keep the gate money, but in subsequent rounds, it was to be shared out amongst the charitable institutions of Derby. In round one, the Alliance enjoyed an 8-1 romp against Derby St. Lukes, thanks to a fine display by brothers J. and H. Brooks, who shared five goals between them. In the semi-final draw, Small Heath were paired with the host club, Derby County, their first meeting since last season's epic F.A. Cup tie. This time the Alliance had a day to forget. First they needed to cope with the non-appearance of goalkeeper, Chris Charsley. Hastily they managed to find a useful substitute, Fred Pitman of County Wanderers, who happened to be in the crowd. Apart from the missing Charsley, the Alliance had sent over their most experienced team for the game, showing the utmost respect to Derby County, and no doubt hoping to show that last season's victory in the F.A cup was no fluke. It meant that there was no place for the rooky Brooks brothers, the heroes of the previous round. Despite bringing their best team, the Alliance were no match for the handy Derby County outfit, losing 3-0.

It was a clear reminder that the Small Heath men were no longer competitive when facing clubs in the higher echelons, unable to keep pace with the improving standards of play. They were being outgunned both in terms of playing strength and financial clout, and drifting down the pecking order. There was a pressing need to get more funds into the club, or face abandoning their professional standing. Behind the scenes, Alf Jones and the rest of the committee were urgently exploring ways to move the club forwards. One report even suggested that a takeover was imminent. The *Athletic News* (12th April 1887) had picked up some gossip that the club was in talks with a "big brewery". Their correspondent wrote, "I hear that there is a likelihood of the Small Heath being taken over by one of the big brewery firms next season, but whether there is any truth in the rumour or not, I am not in a position to say. Time will prove."

Certainly, a precedent had already been set a few months earlier, when Mitchell's Brewery stepped in to help fund the St. George's club. So could this have prompted the idea of a similar arrangement for Small Heath Alliance? As it happened, nothing developed from the rumour, but it still gives rise to the intriguing question of which brewery the Alliance was talking to? It could, again, have been the Mitchell's Brewery, but it seems unlikely that the same brewery would have wished to underpin two local football clubs. The Mitchell's Brewery team had amalgamated with St. George's to form their new alliance, giving it a genuine bond with brewery owner and football beneficiary, Henry Mitchell; something that would have been difficult to replicate with another team.

A more likely scenario is that the "big brewery" referred to in the *Athletic News* was Ansell's Brewery, founded by Joseph Ansell. One of his five sons, publican Alfred Ansell, was an enthusiastic supporter of the Alliance, even serving on the club's committee during the mid-1880s. By coincidence, he had arrived in Small Heath during the same year the Alliance club was formed, moving from the Erdington Arms in Gravelly Hill to the Marquis of Lorne pub in Cattell Road, right in the heart of Alliance territory. Could he have been the key protagonist behind the takeover plans, hoping to play a leading role in running his local club? Rumours of a brewery takeover had surfaced around the same time that Alfred was organising his retirement from business at the age of forty, so perhaps the whole idea was a pet project for when he had more free time. He would undoubtedly have needed to convince his brother William, who, following the death of their father Joseph in 1885, was now in full control of Ansell's Brewery. But how likely was he to support any plans?

A couple of weeks after the rumours first broke, William Ansell was busy initiating his own plans to set up and run a football club. As honorary secretary of Warwickshire Cricket Club, he had called a members' meeting on 30th April, to consider the desirability of adding a football section. The aim was to help cover the £8 weekly running costs of the cricket club in winter, when income was only 30 shillings per week. The proposal received overwhelming support and the Warwick County Football Club was born. Was this the event that finally quashed Alfred Ansell's chance of receiving the support of his brother, who was now committed to the Warwick County club? It's all just conjecture, but it could explain why the rumours of the brewery takeover never materialised, with William Ansell, a one time committee member at Aston Villa (1882) finally ruling out his brother's plans. In the summer of 1887, Alfred Ansell finally left the Marquis of Lorne pub after twelve years, to a swish retirement address at Devon Villa on the Coventry Road.

Another scenario is that the brewery takeover was opposed from within the Alliance committee by Walter Hart, a dedicated teetotaller. If a deal was on the cards, it's highly unlikely that he could have supported it on moral grounds. Could this have been the catalyst for him to come up with the "limited company" idea to inject capital into the club, as an alternative to the brewery takeover? It's an intriguing thought. One project that did move forward during the close season was the scheme to build a large grandstand along the Coventry Road side of the pitch. The enterprising structure would offer mass seating at the venue for the first time, proving that the club still had go-ahead ambitions to compete with the best.

12.3 THE MOVE TO "LIMITED COMPANY" STATUS 1887/88

During the summer of 1887, the hardworking honorary secretary Alf Jones, was re-elected into post for a second season, a vote of confidence for his successful stewardship of the club's first building project. The sizeable new stand was capable of seating a thousand spectators, giving the home crowd a timely boost. Importantly, it would bring increased takings through the gates, giving the committee more scope to attract new players. Early additions included another clutch of players from the Excelsior club, half-back Walter Farley, and forwards Walter Dixon and Chinn.

Amidst this renewed optimism the Alliance soon regained some of their old invincibility, winning their first nine home matches of the season, chalking up victories against Excelsior (twice), Stafford Rangers, Jardines (a Nottingham club), Daventry, Aston Unity, London Casuals, Walsall Town and Burton Wanderers. It was like 'old times' again at Muntz Street, as the Alliance scored thirty goals and conceded only six during the run, but how real was the revival? There was a big question mark against the quality of the opposition, which consistently came from only middle ranking clubs. To be fair to Alf Jones, he was always on the look out for more prestigious opponents, but the club's gradual slide had meant that only middle ranking clubs were now interested in a trip to Small Heath. Even one of their oldest allies, Nottingham Forest, had dropped their fixture with them, the first time in six years.

The unpalatable reality was that each time the Alliance came across a top rated team, defeat inevitably followed. Firstly, West Bromwich Albion dumped them out of the Birmingham Cup, then soon afterwards Aston Villa repeated the deed in the F.A. Cup. This second round encounter was the first meeting between Villa and the Alliance in a competitive fixture, and the fact that Villa were the reigning cup holders only added to the spice. The press noted that "a lot of the Small Heath followers are taking all the odds they can for Small Heath to win" (*Athletic News*, 1st November 1887), yet in reality the Villa club were now far ahead in terms of status and reputation. It had been eight long years since the Alliance's sole victory against them.

Incredibly, by today's standards, the two clubs still went ahead with a pre-planned Monday afternoon friendly at Perry Barr, just twelve days before the historic cup tie. True to form, Villa strolled to a 3-0 win, setting the tone for the big cup match. Unperturbed, the Alliance players went into special training, funded by a generous supporter, determined to break Villa's dominance. There was no such luck. The Alliance slumped to a predictable 4-0 defeat in a game that was all to easy for their rivals. After building their lead, "the Villa rather 'fooled' with their opponents, there being a lot of 'playing pretty', and an evident inclination to show up the Heathens. One could not but admire the Heathens for their hard and gallant fight. They never seemed to lose heart." (*Athletic News*, 8th November 1887).

At this point, the Small Heath club still boasted an undefeated home record, but this would soon be shattered by a fast improving Wolverhampton Wanderers team, who had now broken into the top tier of clubs. Their rise had coincided with the advent of professionalism, enabling them to cream players from nearby amateur clubs. They quashed the Alliance's unbeaten home record with a gritty 3-2 victory. In a heated game, brought on by the over physical play of the Wanderers team, and the intense partisanship of the Small Heath crowd, bonhomie between the players seemed to be in short supply. With no love lost, it was left to the beleaguered referee to sort out the many on-field wrangles and disputes which marred the game. More than once, the referee was forced to halt the game for several minutes, as he battled to restore order and resolve player disputes. Was this an early example of bad sportsmanship caused by the increasing pressures of professionalism, and the influence of the crowd?

As the season progressed, Alf Jones took to advertising for fixtures in the weekly *Athletic News* sports newspaper. It was a free service to help clubs fill vacant dates in their fixture calendar. An advert placed by Jones on the 15th November 1887 read, "Small Heath Alliance want match (away) for Saturday next, November 19th with first class club - send terms to Alfred Jones, 95 Vauxhall Road, Birmingham." It's remarkable, that at such short notice, a match at Oldbury Town Crosswell's resulted. A few clubs had their own telegraph wire, which gave them an immediate communication link. Among them was Wolverhampton Wanderers, whose simple telegraph address was "Wanderers, Wolverhampton". Later, Alf Jones placed another small ad: "Small Heath Alliance want matches at home for December 24, 25 and 31 - Alfred Jones, 95 Vauxhall Road, Birmingham". This time, home matches with Wednesbury Old Athletic (24th) and Rotherham Town (26th) materialised, plus a trip to Grimsby Town on 31st. The latter two were first time opponents, showing that national advertising was bringing about new contact between previously unfamiliar clubs.

Through all of this the problem of the Alliance's teetering finances was still lurking in the background. The brewery takeover rumours had gone quiet, leaving the club back at square one. It was at this stage that committee man, Walter Hart, put forward an idea to raise capital by forming the club into a "limited company". The club would then be run by shareholders, taking away the influence and voting rights of ordinary club members. It was a controversial plan, which faced plenty of opposition from within the club, many of them old players who didn't like the idea of being controlled by shareholders. The democracy of decision making at the club would be changed forever. To some extent, the onset of professionalism had already altered the relationship between players and the club, making them nominal employees, rather than volunteer members involved in it's running. However, the "limited company" idea was seen by many as a step too far, simply giving away control. For the "old school", the idea of handing over the running of "their" club to a group of shareholders, would have been a painful one.

So did Hart need to put his proposal to a ballot of the whole membership, or did he just need to carry a resolution at committee level? No documentation or records exist to reveal how the process unfolded, and newspaper columns from the time seem to be devoid of any information. My instinct is that Hart would have pushed for the final decision to be taken at committee level. This way, he only needed to persuade a majority of his fellow committee men to support his idea. As a respected businessman, and son of an Alderman on the town council, he would have been confident in his ability to win them over, despite the undoubted fierce lobbying from a sizeable group of doubters within the rank and file membership. The doubters had two main bones of contention. Apart from the ceding of control to shareholders, the biggest issue was the proposal to drop the title "Alliance" from the club's name, shortening it to Small Heath F.C. Imagine the heated arguments on this issue alone. The club had always been known as the Alliance, and the thought of removing it from the club's name was unthinkable for some followers and old players. The extent of the furore can only be guessed at.

While all this turmoil and heart searching was going on in Small Heath, dramatic news was about to break across the town in Aston. On 2nd March 1888, William McGregor, an Aston Villa committee member, sent his now famous letter to each of his fellow Villa committee members, and the secretaries of Blackburn Rovers, Bolton Wanderers, Preston North End, Stoke and West Bromwich Albion, suggesting "that ten or twelve of the most prominent clubs in England combine to arrange home-and-away fixtures each season..." These were the first rumblings of the Football League, and the Alliance would soon realise that they were a long way behind this self-proclaimed elite in terms of playing ability and club finances, and were not invited to their discussions. By 17th April, it was all done and dusted. The Football League had been created, consisting of twelve clubs who had formed a type of "closed shop" fixture ring. Undeterred at being cut adrift from this new grouping, Walter Hart soldiered on with his Small Heath shareholder plans. Despite some pockets of opposition within the club, the indications are that the vote in favour came as early as April, when Caesar Jenkyns rejoined the club; surely a sign that the anticipated cash injection from the sale of shares was already being used. Then on 30th April, the club hosted a nostalgic match between a team of 'Past' and a team of 'Present' Alliance players, in a kind of tribute and farewell to the old Alliance club name. The teams were:

Past - W. Rose (goal); Evetts and Elliman (backs); S. Gessey, T. James and F. James (half backs); Howell, Hards (left forwards); Hare (centre); A. James and Davenport (right forwards).
Present – Charsley (goal); Westwood and Barlow (backs); A. Morris, Jenkyns and A. Simms (half backs); T. Hill and C. Simms (left forwards); A. Smith (centre); Stanley and Weetman (right forwards).

In May, another highly rated player was brought in, with striker Will Devey secured from Aston Unity. His arrival coincided with the abrupt exit of captain Austin Smith, who had apparently upset the club committee. Could the dispute have been linked to the shareholder takeover? Even though Smith had only been at Muntz Street for one season, his departure was a big surprise, particularly after his prolific goal scoring record. Thankfully, Will Devey was a fine replacement, both as a goal scorer and captain, becoming a firm favourite with the crowd over the next three seasons. It was rumoured that he was paid 12/6d per week to sign, probably the highest pay of any Small Heath player during this period. His debut came in the club's last game as Small Heath Alliance, a match against Aston Villa on 14th May 1888. The game drew a crowd of three thousand to Muntz Street, who witnessed a disappointing 4-1 defeat to bring the curtain down on the Small Heath Alliance era. The last team to represent the Alliance was:

Chris Charsley (goal); Westwood and Barlow (backs); A. Morris, Caesar Jenkyns and Alf Simms (half backs); George Short, Tom Davenport (right forwards); Will Devey (centre); Eddie Stanley, Ted Hill (left forwards).

Walter Hart and William McGregor (seated) in 1903

In the week before the Villa game, Walter Hart had suffered a personal tragedy, with the sudden death of his father, Alderman Matthew J. Hart, at home in Grange Road, Small Heath. He had fallen ill following a business trip to Glasgow, and died on 9th May. It was a difficult time for Walter, having to deal with both his family bereavement, and the final arrangements for "limited company" status. There was also the distraction of William McGregor's Football League project, which was now all decided. If Walter Hart had been hoping to use the Villa match as a chance to discuss progress with McGregor, and make a last ditch plea to be included, it was now far too late. Ironically, it was probably McGregor who wanted to talk to Hart about his trailblazing shareholder plans.

The onset of professionalism had created an issue of who technically employed the players. They couldn't be bound to their "clubs", simply because clubs were not classed as corporate bodies. For McGregor at Villa, it currently meant that the club's twenty four professionals were, in effect, legally bound to him and the two other lessees of Villa's Perry Barr ground. Hart's "limited company" approach would help put things on a firmer footing by making the players employees of any newly constituted company board, something McGregor felt had merit.

It's also possible that McGregor had other motives. For a time he had been anxious about the overbearing influence of George Kynoch, a co-lessee of the Perry Barr ground, and club president. Kynoch was a larger than life personality, fond of the high life, and quite domineering. After generating vast wealth from his Lion Works ammunitions business, he had been elected as president of the Aston Manor Conservative Association in March 1885, and then in July the following year became the local M.P. With his wealth, status and influence, he was almost uncontrollable, something that McGregor loathed. The pair were polar opposites in terms of temperament and disposition. McGregor was a quiet man, preferring a more considered approach, and sticking to protocol.

It's possible, therefore, that McGregor was viewing the "limited company" idea as a way of controlling Kynoch's autocratic tendencies. Certainly, the circumstantial evidence points to this. One clue was McGregor's preference that no member could hold more than two shares. As things turned out, McGregor didn't need to worry. In November 1888, Kynoch took flight to South Africa, amidst tales of mounting business debts and ill health. Soon afterwards Villa's plans for "limited company" status were quietly shelved. Were the two events linked? We shall never know. As for Kynoch, he never returned to Britain, passing away in Johannesburg in February 1891, after a long struggle with cancer. He died in relative poverty, running a gun store, still technically the M.P. for Aston Manor. It wasn't until several years later in 1896, that Villa eventually embarked on the "limited company" option, in tandem with their move to Aston Lower Grounds.

12.4 THE WORLD'S FIRST FOOTBALL CLUB SHAREHOLDERS

Small Heath Alliance was formally registered as "Small Heath Football Club Limited" on 24th July 1888, becoming the first football club in the world to be owned and run by shareholders. It was an event that "startled" the football world. (*The Sheffield Independent,* 22nd December 1888). In total, 216 shares were issued, raising around £650 in share capital for the club. Each individual was allowed to buy as many shares as they wanted, but as a safety measure, the maximum number of votes per shareholder was restricted to a maximum of five. The voting restriction was introduced to allay fears that the club could otherwise be dominated by a few wealthy individuals.

The first board of directors was:
    Edwin William Badland
    Thomas Denston
    Walter Dormer
    Walter William Hart (chairman)
    Alfred Reuben Jones
    John Campbell Orr
    J. Smith
    William Starling and Herbert Everton Greatorex
    (honorary secretaries – unpaid)

The most notable feature was the absence of any former players. Hart himself had made a single first team appearance back in 1880, but this hardly qualified him as their representative. In reality, the changes sidelined many former players who found it difficult to come to terms with the shareholding idea. There is a suspicion that several club founders, such as the Edden brothers, drifted away at this time, feeling alienated from the club they had once created. Walter Hart, the architect of the plans, was inevitably appointed as the first chairman of the board, with the duo William Starling and Herbert Greatorex given the posts of honorary secretaries. Previously, it had been traditional for one secretary to run first team affairs, and the other to look after second team matters. Once the new structure was in place, it seems that Starling took responsibility for match affairs, and Greatorex, an accounts clerk by occupation, the club finances. The experienced William Starling had served a previous stint during the early 1880s. Alf Jones, the immediate past secretary(86/87 and 87/88), was now a shareholder with a seat on the board, an obvious indication of his support for Hart's controversial plans.

The most prominent businessman on the board was Edwin William Badland, a wealthy coal merchant, whose business operated on a massive scale. His original base was at the Palmer Street Wharf, just off Watery Lane on the Birmingham and Warwick Canal, where his coal was unloaded from barges and stored. He also occupied railway sidings at the wharf in Fazeley Street dedicated to receiving a constant stream of coal deliveries by train. The coal wagons were emblazoned with his name, Edwin W. Badland. Even today, the Hornby Model Railway company produces replicas of his coal wagons, complete with his logo.

Other inaugural board members were Walter Dormer, a glass salesman from Golden Hillock Road, Tom Denston, a solicitor's clerk who, during the early 1880s, had been honorary secretary of Small Heath Swifts F.C., and J. Smith, whose identity has yet to be discovered. Denston would later become the club's first paid official in mid-1892, when he was elected to the post of paid secretary. He didn't last long, being replaced by Alf Jones in October 1892. The biggest surprise was the appearance of John Campbell Orr, the secretary of the Birmingham And District F.A. on the board. He obviously saw no conflict of interest caused by having a financial interest in one of his member clubs.

Whether William Hart had sought approval from the Football Association before proceeding with his shareholder plans isn't clear. When Preston North End, for example, followed a similar path four years later in 1892, they first applied to the F.A., who gave agreement on the proviso that "dividends must be limited to 5% of the value of the shares." This happened to be the same dividend level paid out by the "Small Heath Football Club Limited" in July 1889 after the first year of trading, which might suggest that the F.A. had indeed been consulted by Hart and imposed the same 5% dividend limit; either that or it was just a coincidence. The club retained the

Small Heath name until 1st August 1905, when it was changed to Birmingham Football Club. Finally, in the summer of 1943, it became Birmingham City Football Club.

APPENDIX 1

SMALL HEATH ALLIANCE COMPETITIVE MATCHES
(Alliance score given first)

1878/79
Birmingham Cup
Round 1 - Calthorpe (h) 0-1 (9th November 1878)

1879/80
Birmingham Cup
Round 1 - Wednesbury Old Athletic (a) 2-1 (25th October 1879)
Round 2 - Aston Unity (h) 1-1 (13th December 1879)
Replay   - Aston Unity (a) 3-5 (20th December 1879)

1880/81
Birmingham Cup
Round 1 - Stoke (h) 6-1 (13th November 1880)
Round 2 - Bye
Round 3 - Aston Unity (h) 6-4 (29th January 1881)
Round 4 - Walsall Swifts (n, Lower Grounds) 2-2 (12th February 1881)
Replay   - Walsall Swifts (n, Lower Grounds) 0-4 (12th March 1881)

1881/82
Birmingham Cup
Round 1 - Aston Clifton (h) 7-2 (12th November 1881)
Round 2 - Wednesbury Old Athletic (h) 2-7 (17th December 1881)

F.A.Cup
Round 1 - Derby Town (h) 4-1 (5th November 1881)
Round 2 - Wednesbury Old Athletic (a) 0-6 (3rd December 1881)

Walsall Cup
Round 1 - Aston Unity (a) 3-0 (26th November 1881)
Round 2 - Wednesbury Old Athletic (a) 1-5 (31st December 1881)

Wednesbury Charity Cup
Round 1 - Wellington (h) 2-2 (19th November 1881)
Replay   - Wellington (a) 3-0 (10th December 1881)
S-Final - Wednesbury Old Athletic, lost (6th May 1882)
           (Score and venue unknown)

1882/83
Birmingham Cup
Round 1 - Walsall Town (a) 0-1 (11th November 1882)

F.A.Cup
Round 1 - Stafford Road Works (h) 3-3 (4th November 1882)
Replay   - Stafford Road Works (a) 2-6 (18th November 1882)

Walsall Cup
Round 1 - Bye
Round 2 - Pelsall Rovers (h) 3-0 (2nd December 1882)
Round 3 - Darlastan All Saints (h) 16-0 (27th January 1883)
S-Final - St. George's (n, Wellington Rd.) 1-0 (3rd March 1883)
Final   - Wednesbury Old Athletic (n, Chuckery) 4-1 (31st March 1883)

1883/84
Birmingham Cup
Round 1 - Brownhills (a) 4-2 (27th October 1883)
Round 2 - Dudley (h) 11-0 (1st December 1883)
Round 3 - Walsall Swifts (h) 2-2 (5th January 1884)
Replay   - Walsall Swifts (a) 0-2 (12th January 1884)

F.A.Cup
Round 1 - Excelsior (h) 1-1 (20th October 1883)
Replay   - Excelsior (a) 2-3 (10th November 1883)

Walsall Cup
Round 1 - Wednesbury Old Athletic (a) 1-2 (3rd November 1883)

Wednesbury Charity Cup
Round 2 - Nottingham Forest, lost (score, venue and date unknown)

1884/85
Birmingham Cup
Round 1 - Stafford Rangers (a) 1-0 (18th October 1884)
Round 2 - Excelsior (h) 2-1 (29th November 1884)
Replay(after protest) - Excelsior (h) 3-5 (29th December 1884)

F.A.Cup
Round 1 - Excelsior (a) 0-2 (8th November 1884)

1885/86
Birmingham Cup
Round 1 - Sandwell (a) 3-3 (10th October 1885)
Replay   - Sandwell (h)10-3 (17th October 1885)
Round 2 - Wednesbury Old Athletic (h) 3-3 (14th November 1885)
Replay   - Wednesbury Old Athletic (a) 1-3 (28th November 1885)

Birmingham Charity Cup
Round 1 - Aston Unity (n, at Lower Grounds) 2-5 (20th March 1886)

F.A.Cup
Round 1 - Burton Wanderers (h) 9-2 (31st October 1885)
Round 2 - Darwen (h) 3-1 (21st November 1885)
Round 3 - Derby County (h) 4-2 (12th December 1885)
Round 4 - Bye
Round 5 - Davenham (h) 2-1 (16th January 1886)
Round 6 - Redcar (h) 2-0 (13th February 1886)
S/Final   - W.B.A. (n, Lower Grounds) 0-4 (6th March 1886)

1886/87
Birmingham Cup
Round 1 - Stafford Road Works (h) 7-0 (9th October 1886)
Round 2 - Bye
Round 3 - Coseley (h) 13-0 (4th December 1886)
Round 4 - Derby Junction (h) 4-0 (15th January 1887)
Replay after protest (frozen pitch) - Derby Junction (h) 1-0 (22nd January 1887)
S/Final   - Long Eaton Rangers (n, Lower Grounds) 2-2 (12th March 1887)
Replay   - Long Eaton Rangers (n) 0-2 (21st March 1887)

Derby County Charity Cup
Round 1 - Derby St. Lukes (h) 8-1 (26th March 1887)
S/Final   - Derby County (a) 0-3 (30th April 1887)

F.A.Cup
Round 1 - Mitchell's St. George's (h) 1-3 (30th October 1887)

Walsall Cup
Round 1 - Walsall Swifts (h) 2-0 (23rd October 1886)
Round 2 - W.B.A. (h) 0-3 (27th November 1886)

1887/88
Birmingham Cup
Round 1 - W.B.A. (a) 0-2 (8th October 1887)

Birmingham Charity Cup
Round 1 - Mitchell's St. George's (n, Wellington Rd.) 1-3 (4th April 1888)

F.A.Cup
Round 1 - Aston Unity (h) 6-1 (15th October 1887)
Round 2 - Aston Villa (a) 0-4 (5th November 1887)

Walsall Cup
Round 1 - Mitchell's St. George's (h) 2-5 (8th October 1887). Both clubs played their reserve teams, as their first teams were playing ties in round one of the Birmingham Cup.

APPENDIX 2

ALLIANCE PLAYERS' REPRESENTATIVE APPEARANCES FOR THE BIRMINGHAM AND DISTRICT FOOTBALL ASSOCIATION 1875-1888 (B.&D.F.A. score given first)

Billy Edden
1. v London F.A. at Kennington Oval, 0-8 (30th November 1878)
2. v Sheffield Association at Bramhall Lane, Sheffield, 0-10 (14th December 1878)
3. v Scotch Counties at Cathkin Park, 0-6 (19th February 1881)

Arthur James
1. v Sheffield Association at Bramhall Lane, 0-10 (14th December 1878)
2. v Scotch Counties at Hampden Park, 1-7 (18th January 1879)
3. v Scotch Counties at Aston Lower Grounds, 3-4 (15th March 1879)
4. v Lancashire Association at Aston Lower Grounds, 7-2 (27th December 1880) First match between the two.
5. v Scotch Counties at Cathkin Park, 0-6 (19th February 1881)
6. v England XI at Aston Lower Grounds, 4-5 (5th March 1881)
7. v London F.A. at Kennington Oval, 1-1 (29th October 1881)
8. v Lancashire F.A. at Darwen, 3-4 (3rd December 1881)
   Arthur James scored one.
9. v Sheffield Assoc. at Aston Lower Grounds, 2-1 (26th December 1881)
   Arthur James scored the winner.
10. v Scotch Counties at Aston Lower Grounds, 3-1 (25th February 1882)

Chris Charsley
1. v London F.A. at Perry Barr, 3-0 (2nd April 1887)
2. v London F.A. at Kennington Oval, 5-0 (4th February 1888)
3. v Cheshire Association at the Alexandra Ground, Crewe, 6-1 (26th March 1888)

Other Game
For a representative game on 26th December 1883, between a Birmingham "Town Men" XI and a Rest of the District team, including representatives from Wellington, Wolverhampton, Wednesbury and Walsall, the Alliance club supplied five players for the "Town Men". These were "Jumbo" Taylor (back), Fred James (half-back), W. Jones (centre forward), Arthur James and Eddie Stanley (right wings). The game was organised by the Birmingham and District F.A. at Aston Lower Grounds and played in front of two thousand spectators. The "Town Men" triumphed 4-1 against only ten men.

APPENDIX 3

CLUB CAPTAINS

Twenty-one year old **Billy Edmonds** is attributed as the club's first captain, as recorded by William McGregor in the 1906 *Book of Football*. By the following season, 1876/77, **Tom James**, the eldest of the three James brothers, had stepped into the role (The *Sport and Play* journal, 14th March 1877). During this period the team played to Sheffield Rules, usually 12 aside.

In 1878, Tom's younger brother Arthur became captain. **Arthur James** was the club's best player and one of the most eye-catching forwards in the district. No-one ran faster with the ball at their feet, and it was during the 1878/79 season that he was first selected for the Birmingham and District F.A. team. When he was away on representative duty, **William Penfield** would deputise for him, and from 1880/81, **Bill Slater** would step in. **Arthur James'** captaincy spanned a period of eight years. He was revered by the Small Heath faithful and completely loyal to his club. However, his spell in charge was littered with bad luck, cruelly missing out on the Alliance's two finest cup runs due to injury.

He was forced to sit out the whole of the triumphant Walsall Cup campaign in 1882/83, after sustaining life threatening injuries during a game at Ruabon Druids in October 1882. As the Alliance's most dangerous forward, he had been deliberately targeted for rough treatment and reckless charging. The internal injuries he suffered left him incapacitated for the whole season, forcing him to miss out on the Alliance's first trophy success. For Arthur, it must have been an evening of mixed emotions, watching his stand-in **Bill Slater** being presented with the Walsall Cup at the Priory Hotel, Walsall in May 1883.

Arthur returned to action as captain for the start of the 1883/84 season, before more bad luck followed. In a Birmingham Cup tie at Walsall Swifts in January 1884, he was kicked on the jaw leaving him out cold. No bones were broken, but a whiplash type injury to his neck had left it's toll. He carried on for one more full season, before bowing out just as the Alliance were on the cusp of their famous F.A. Cup run in 1885/86. He was captain for the 9-2 first round victory against Burton Wanderers, but sadly missed out on the Alliance's epic run. The man who took over was **John "Jack" Hare**, a tough no nonsense defender, who led the team through to the semi-final. He was captain for nearly two seasons, then in February 1887 Arthur James made a surprise four game comeback, which included a Birmingham Cup semi-final appearance at Aston Lower Grounds. He soon realised though that the physical demands were too much for him, and he retired for the second time.

For the 1887/88 season, the last under the Small Heath Alliance name, **Austin Smith**, a free scoring centre forward, was appointed captain.

APPENDIX 4

HONORARY SECRETARIES

The early years of the club's running are shrouded in mystery, as it appears that no minute books from the Alliance era have survived. Folklore suggests that Billy Edmonds was the first honorary secretary, but as he is also recorded as the club's first football captain, it seems doubtful that he would have combined both roles simultaneously. Some modern day accounts have speculated that Arthur James signed the paperwork to rent the Muntz Street enclosure in 1877, which could suggest that he was an early incumbent.

The following is a list of known honorary secretaries pieced together from contemporary or near contemporary sources. However it only starts in 1879, and there are still a few gaps.

1879/80 - William Edden
1880/81 - ?
1881/82 - Philip William Harlow
1882/83 - William Samuel Starling
1883/84 - ? possibly William Starling
1884/85 - Sam Gessey
1885/86 - Walter William Hart
1886/87 - Alfred Reuben Jones
1887/88 - Alfred Reuben Jones

REFERENCE SOURCES

Most sources are referenced in the text throughout the book. The following publications were also useful sources of background information, as were census records and various births, marriages and deaths records.

Mike Bradbury - Lost Teams of the Midlands (2013)
Steve Carr - The History of the Birmingham Senior Cup 1876-1905 (n.d)
Steve Carr - The Old Uns, The Story of Wednesbury Old Athletic F.C. 1874-1893 (n.d)
Graham Curry - Early Sheffield Football, A Source Book (2013)
Tony Matthews - Birmingham City The Complete Record (1989 & 2010)
Tony Matthews - The Encyclopaedia of Birmingham City Football Club 1875-2000 (2000)
Richard Sanders - Beastly Fury, The Strange Birth of British Football (2009)

Front cover photograph: *The earliest known image of the Small Heath Alliance team, circa 1884. The player with his foot on the ball is captain Arthur James.*

Back cover photograph: *The Plume of Feathers pub in Miles Street, Small Heath as it was in the mid-1970s. The pub was the club's early headquarters. Sadly it has since been demolished. (photo courtesy of Richard Wood).*